Civil Society and Local Ownership in the Global South

This book assesses local civil society responses to conflict, militarism, climate change, and disease in the global south.

Grounded in empirical analyses of civil society developments in Sub-Saharan African countries, Jordan, Lebanon, Yemen, Palestine, and Syria, the book demonstrates that civil society organisations in unstable circumstances and divided societies have room and power to help and influence their societies and to become engaged in supporting active participation in society to help communities to endure uncertainty. The book considers the ways in which crises of conflict, war, climate change, and disease have challenged civil society organisations in their scope of work and operations. It also demonstrates the benefits of local ownership and grassroots initiatives in helping to empower local people by contributing to decision-making processes in peacebuilding and post-conflict consensus-building.

This book will be an important read for researchers looking for a new approach to civil society in a global south context, by focusing on local ownership and the different perspectives for each country, in terms of leadership culture and development in practice.

Ibrahim Natil is an associate professor of international relations at Joaan Bin Jassim Academy; a visiting professor/lecturer at the University of Law, Business School, UK; and a research fellow at Dublin City University, Ireland. He has been the co-convenor of NGOs in the Development Study Group at DSA-UK since 2018 and was elected recently as a council member of the Development Study Association UK (2024–2027).

Routledge Explorations in Development Studies

This Development Studies series features innovative and original research at the regional and global scale. It promotes interdisciplinary scholarly works drawing on a wide spectrum of subject areas, in particular politics, health, economics, rural and urban studies, sociology, environment, anthropology, and conflict studies.

Topics of particular interest are globalization; emerging powers; children and youth; cities; education; media and communication; technology development; and climate change.

In terms of theory and method, rather than basing itself on any orthodoxy, the series draws broadly on the tool kit of the social sciences in general, emphasizing comparison, the analysis of the structure and processes, and the application of qualitative and quantitative methods.

Arts-based Research in Global Development
Performing Knowledge
Edited by Vicki-Ann Ware, Kirsten Sadeghi-Yekta, Tim Prentki, and Wasim al Kurdi

Youth Voice and Participatory Arts in Global Development
The May Group

Human Rights and the United Nations
Paradox and Promise
Edited by Abigail B. Bakan and Yasmeen Abu-Laban

Civil Society and Local Ownership in the Global South
Responses to Conflict and Militarism
Edited by Ibrahim Natil

For more information about this series, please visit: www.routledge.com/Routledge-Explorations-in-Development-Studies/book-series/REDS

Civil Society and Local Ownership in the Global South

Responses to Conflict and Militarism

Edited by Ibrahim Natil

LONDON AND NEW YORK

First published 2025
by Routledge
4 Park Square, Milton Park, Abingdon, Oxon OX14 4RN

and by Routledge
605 Third Avenue, New York, NY 10158

Routledge is an imprint of the Taylor & Francis Group, an informa business

British Library Cataloguing-in-Publication Data
A catalogue record for this book is available from the British Library

ISBN: 978-1-032-93241-5 (hbk)
ISBN: 978-1-032-93243-9 (pbk)
ISBN: 978-1-003-56504-8 (ebk)

DOI: 10.4324/9781003565048

Typeset in Times New Roman
by Apex CoVantage, LLC

Contents

Contributors

Ghazi Al-Assaf is Associate Professor of Defence Economics and Associate Dean for Scientific Research Affairs at Joaan Bin Jassim Academy for Defence Studies and Associate Professor of Economics at the University of Jordan, Amman, Jordan.

Hani Albasoos is Associate Professor of Security and Strategic Studies at Joaan Bin Jassim Academy for Defence Studies. He has also worked for a number of academic institutions in Palestine, Oman, and Qatar since 2006.

Ahmed El Assal is a doctoral candidate and Marie Skłodowska-Curie Research Fellow at the International Institute of Social Studies (ISS), Erasmus University Rotterdam, Rotterdam, the Netherlands. He holds an MA degree in governance, development, and public policy, University of Sussex, East Sussex, England.

Nguh Nwei Asanga Fon is a researcher, civil society leader, and consultant. Dr Fon is Executive Director of the Community Awareness and Development Association Cameroon (CADAC) and is a lecturer at the International Leadership University, Yaoundé, Cameroon.

Sali Hafez holds a Master of Health Science in Global Health from the University of Tampere in Finland and a bachelor's degree from Alexandria University, Alexandria, Egypt. She is a doctoral candidate in public health policy at the London School for Hygiene & Tropical Medicine, UK.

Ibrahim Natil published 8 books and more than 60 papers and chapters and worked for a number of institutions at different levels, including teaching, researching, grants management, leadership, and external examiner/supervising PhD and MA students.

Beata Piskorska is Vice-Rector of the John Paul II Catholic University of Lublin for Students and Internationalisation. She is an expert of Team Europe at the European Commission Representation in Poland and the president of the Association for Education and International Research.

1 Introducing and Exploring New Concepts and Practice of Local Ownership

Ibrahim Natil

Introduction

This book enriches the current debate on civil society organisations' (CSOs) contributions; service delivery; and response(s) to conflicts, wars, militarism, climate change, and diseases in the global south. It provides the reader with empirically based and up-to-date but scientifically grounded analyses of civil society developments in global south countries such as Sudan and Sub-Saharan African countries, Jordan, Lebanon, Yemen, Palestine, and Syria, in response to various challenges caused by conflicts, wars, militarism, climate change, and diseases. It appeals not only to an academic audience but also to international agencies, policymakers, and practitioners active in the specified regions. It investigates important questions, including: To what extent have conflicts, wars, and militarism challenged CSOs' scope of work, operations, and missions in conflict zones? What are the impacts of conflicts and militarism on CSOs' shifts and challenges? The author has included this theoretical chapter specifically to provide balance.

The other chapters are empirical, but the following chapters all discuss the theories and methodologies relevant to the country's case studies. Therefore, the balance between theoretical/methodological and empirical discussions is ensured. This introductory chapter is included to provide sound theoretical and structural guidance for the reader in which to place each case study. The introduction also places the scope of the book into the wider framework of the academic discussion about the topic, providing clear references to related materials and themes. The book focuses on CSOs' local ownership in responding to current challenges caused by conflicts, militarism, climate change, and diseases. Bojicic-Dzelilovic and Martin (2016) have previously discussed how "local ownership" is an important issue for international actors and donors. CSOs attempt to show the advantages of different groups working for mutual benefit with tangible results when engaging in grassroots cultural,

DOI: 10.4324/9781003565048-1

social, and political activities. There are different definitions for CSOs; however, Asian Development Bank defines CSOs as:

> Civil society organizations (CSOs) are non-state actors whose aims are neither to generate profits nor to seek governing power. CSOs unite people to advance shared goals and interests. They have a presence in public life, expressing the interests and values of their members or others, and are based on ethical, cultural, scientific, religious, or philanthropic considerations. CSOs include nongovernment organizations (NGOs), professional associations, foundations, independent research institutes, community-based organizations (CBOs), faith-based organizations, people's organizations, social movements, and labor unions.
>
> (Asian Development Bank 2009)

As Donais (2012) has discussed, CSOs' grassroots activities may empower local people's contribution to decision-making processes in terms of peacebuilding and local ownership post-conflict consensus-building. Furthermore, the participatory process is also associated with the practice of a top-down mechanism conducted to include citizens' engagement with and contribution to the public sector, as Bherer, Dufour, and Montambeault (2016) argue. In addition, the book considers the viewpoints and experiences of local communities, activists, and individuals who are directly affected by these problems. Furthermore, an exclusive emphasis on the influence of external variables such as conflicts and climate change may overlook the significance of internal governance and financial frameworks in determining CSOs' activities in these particular areas. The book's central argument, however, indicates that CSOs in unstable circumstances and divided societies have room and power to help and influence their society and become engaged in developing society and support active participation therein to endure uncertainty, shifts, and challenges.

This book, however, studies these challenges and how CSOs have coped with these shifts, and it also examines at least two different CSOs from each country to identify the differences among various cultural contexts, political environments, and social dynamics to understand these shifts and challenges. For example societies in Sudan, Libya, Yemen, Lebanon, Palestine. and Syria have been enduring very severe circumstances owing to economic declines, the absence of reconciliation, and violence/militarism. These circumstances have already created barriers to effective CSOs. This chapter also provides for the selection of theoretical and methodological frameworks for each country's case study. The editor provides the readers with a more detailed rationale for these choices. This presents a general overview of the academic discourse on the topic by focusing on specific examples to illustrate key points in the volume. This focuses on both the theoretical and methodological frameworks, as well as empirical examples.

The editor introduces a clear definition: despite operating in restrictive political environments and navigating the complexities of conflicts, civil wars, and diseases, civil society organisations (CSOs) have shown remarkable resilience. In other words, the editor introduces a new concept of local ownership through a selective literature review by exploring evidence that CSOs have made significant adaptations to ensure their survival during times of crisis and conflicts. This can be done by analysing CSOs activities, work delivered, and statements produced by CSO representatives to emphasise on the invaluable contributions they make to their communities.

The contributors interviewed CSO activists and leaders to explore the challenges they face and the innovative strategies they employ to continue their crucial work in challenging circumstances. It examines, for example, some CSOs which have successfully adjusted and broadened their range of activities to address conflicts, wars, and militarism while cooperating effectively with international organizations, policymakers, and practitioners to tackle these problems and amplify their influence in practical settings. Despite the fact of these challenges, this case illustrates CSOs as drivers for creativity and cooperation while functioning in a complicated social, political, and economic environment.

New Examples of Local Ownership

To explore new examples of local ownership of civil society, this volume brings some case studies from various places around the world (Sudan, Sub-Saharan African countries, Jordan, Lebanon, Yemen, Palestine, and Syria) to highlight the challenges and opportunities in responding to conflict and militarism. To what extent do CSOs engage in local ownership activities? What is the relationship between local target groups and CSOs? What are the distinctive dimensions of development and local ownership, if any? Which innovative/alternative forms might CSOs take in terms of responding to wars and conflict? The chapters in this book seek to answer these and other questions. Therefore, the volume explores new practices of how CSOs in such countries are shaped by and react while responding to conflicts and militarism. It also provides up-to-date analysis of local grassroots organisations and civil society groups from Sudan, Sub-Saharan African countries, Jordan, Lebanon, Yemen, Palestine, and Syria. The contributors have enriched debate, analysis, and discussion by delivering academic pieces by reflecting various experiences from various perspectives and contexts, particularly from the global south.

The chapters are structured around the demonstrated CSOs' theme, values, and concept of local ownership in countries of global south action, and they are further subdivided into 'local ownership' and 'different examples of civil society responses' to make the edited volume more coherent. It discusses a number of definitions in reference to local ownership in terms of social, culture, and development contexts. It is divided into eight chapters, which are grouped together by the themes: local ownership in the global south and responses of grassroots civil society to conflict and militarism. Natil's theoretical chapter in this volume specifically is for the purpose of providing this balance. It introduces the theoretical framework, exploring the technical constraints imposed by conflicts, militarism, climate change, and diseases, their impact(s) on CSOs' service delivery, and how these can be understood. These also assist in understanding: To what extent has the donors' shifting agenda affected CSOs' local initiatives? The CSOs' leadership are aware of donors' shifts and values at their local level. To what extent have the CSOs understood the donors' values at their local activities?

The other chapters are empirical, but each chapter also discusses the theories and methodologies relevant to its country case study. Therefore, the balance between theoretical/methodological and empirical discussions is ensured. For example Natil's chapter introduces the explorations of CSOs' local ownership and the responses of civil society to harsh circumstances such as conflicts, militarism, and wars. This includes examining new practices of civil society grassroots groups in which they work and sheds light on their shifts and adaptation in contemporary societies. It includes the background, framework, scope, and questions of volume and methods. It focuses on the theme of CSOs' responses by examining specific case studies, aiming at improving our understanding of the local ownership concepts and practices of CSOs' activities in various societies in the global south and their relationship with partners in the global north. Natil's introductory chapter and conclusion provide a sound theoretical and structural guidance for the reader in which to place each individual case study chapter. For example Society Voice Foundation (SVF) in Palestine works in close cooperation and partnership with a network of local CSOs to select target groups of women to be trained as agents for local peace-making in accordance with certain criteria, including openness, willingness to practise their skills, experiences, and the values of CSOs' missions and values. These CSOs are engaged with local activists to design, lead, and/or evaluate peacebuilding actions. Young activists from women's CSOs have also engaged in forming local networks, groups, or structures to help local volunteers who are trained by SVF in Palestine on peacebuilding programmes funded by international donors from EU countries (2011–2022) to put their newly acquired skills into practice. These networks or structures include community education tools and approaches to promoting women's role in local peacebuilding, community development, and human rights programmes. However, local CSOs had to confirm how to sustain this local ownership after the project's completion by replying to this question: "Explain how sustainability will be secured after completion of the action. This can include aspects of necessary measures and strategies built into the action, follow-up activities, ownership by target groups".

As a part of the project's implementation, SVF had to work on strengthening cooperation, communication, and cross-fertilisation between the target group, the policymakers and the CSOs participating as a part of local ownership. It also set up an advisory committee from the local community to assist in conducting and implementing peacebuilding activities. The project was aimed at empowering the capacities of local peacebuilding agents like young women in lobbying, networking, and organisation to influence decision-makers much more powerfully to increase peacebuilding. These organisations will continue their operations within the network created by the project to stand as promoters and watchdogs of peacebuilding practices based on accountability and transparency. SVF's leaders also had to confirm local ownership in responding to the question, "How will the project change the attitudes of all stakeholders towards the action in general and the activities in particular?" Natil (2021, 2022, 2023).

The introduction and conclusion also place the scope of the book into the wider framework of the academic discussion about the topic, so there is clear reference to related materials and themes within which this volume is situated. Natil also presents the extent to which civil society activists and leaders launch initiatives to assist their locals despite wars, violent conflict, harsh economic circumstances, and the complexity of their local political environment as (Natil, Malila, and Sai 2020). It also discusses the development process of local ownership concepts and practices by providing the readers a new concept of these definitions. For example *Sali Hafez and Ahmed El Assal discuss* local and organisational complexities facing CSOs in five Arab countries such as Jordan, Lebanon, Syria, Yemen, and Palestine Arab countries while implementing safeguarding measures among them in Chapter 2.

Challenges to Local Ownership

Wars and violent conflicts represent a crucial challenge and barriers to local and national ownership. These complexities include the factors influencing local responses to humanitarian crises by focusing on implementing safeguarding measures among CSOs. This chapter also presents these challenges, which are defined as CSOs' power to cope with conflict, a lack of policies, a restrictive political environment, with the complexity of conflict, civil wars, and diseases and their impact on the sociocultural and economic contexts. The editor reviews selective literature to explore CSOs' adaptations made during the wars and conflicts to keep their organisations alive. The chapter also analyses CSOs' activities, work delivered, and statements and literature produced by their representatives and activists. This analysis is partially based on the author's interviews with some civil society activists who engaged in activities during periods of conflicts, civil wars, and diseases.

In this context, the contributors have sought to assist readers to understand the adopted measures taken by local humanitarian CSOs to ensure the enforcement of safeguarding policies in the long run. Nguh answers the questions of civil society local ownership in Africa in Chapter 3. Nguh also explains in detail the idea of humanity's army as used in the title. Although civil society organizations (CSOs) in Sub-Saharan Africa have undeniably made significant progress in effectively addressing humanitarian crises, the author examines the potential constraints and deficiencies that may impede their endeavours, such as resource constraints, coordination challenges, and the possibility of internal corruption within these organisations. The author, however, explores the significance of government and international relief agencies in delivering help and support in times of humanitarian crises, as civil society organisations (CSOs) in isolation may lack the capability to adequately address the multifaceted needs of the impacted people.

From a different perspective, Hani Albasoos discusses, in Chapter 4, some local civil society's engagement in delivering humanitarian assistance in cooperation with Qatari diplomacy to the Gaza Strip. This analysis shows that wars are a real threat to local civil society lives despite frequent global initiatives and UN's calls to end the armed conflict to save lives, tackle the humanitarian crisis, and facilitate delivering critical humanitarian supplies on different occasions to local communities. Local coordination and collaboration, among various civil society groups, have been always affected in the conflict zones. Local societies face inhuman conditions in conflict zones where services, infrastructure, and healthcare facilities are rare *as* Natil (2023) discusses. Collaboration between formal institutions and CSOs, however, is one of the core approaches in conflict areas while tackling the humanitarian crisis. Beata Piskorska explains in Chapter 5, however, the EU's approach to accommodate global challenges in the form of humanitarian crises such as security issues, conflicts, climate, and diseases. Piskorska also examines EU's strategies and external activities in responding to various crises by defining the concept of variation in the quality of the EU's changes across the EU's existing strategy.

This engagement delivers an in-depth analysis to understand the notion of international actors' shifts in an appropriate context. This will assist the readers to understand the EU's external activities globally. It also can be influenced by factors such as external pressures and geopolitical issues in controlling their classical approach of intervention such as the EU and their engagement with local civil society actors in the global south. The author, however, examines the EU's external activity towards the migrant crisis, where member states lacked coordination in finding a unified solution and instead opted for independent border control measures. This lack of cohesion posed a significant obstacle to the EU's ability to adapt to new circumstances. For example, EU has used digital diplomacy to implement its activities and engaging with civil society organisations in the global south as Natil (2023) discusses themes of public diplomacy and CSOs.

In responding to these challenges facing the civil society in the global south, the book also indicates that the significant use of digital technology tools and in their impact on delivering local actions at different levels. This includes communicating their values and engaging with various target groups. In this context, Snow and Cull (2020) confirm the importance of digital use to engaging with public corporations. CSOs use technology in responding to various crises. In addition to this, technology is used to get engaged with foreign donors and international partners. This indicates the questions: To what extent has digital technology affected local CSOs engaging with foreign donors and international partners in times of crises such as conflict and violence? How have CSOs employed digital technology tools in responding to shifting landscapes, owing to conflict and violence? Alexander (2018) discusses the use of digital technology which remains a significant tool of soft power for public activities including CSOs' operations in the field of development.

The book provides the reader with empirically based and up-to-date but scientifically grounded analyses of civil society developments in the global south countries. Natil's chapter (Chapter 6) studies the barriers facing CSOs and their local human rights defenders and peacebuilders activists in Libya and the impact of political division, violence, and the absence of united government on their local delivery, intervention, and operations at grassroots levels. It also explains to what extent women's CSOs contributed to local peacebuilding processes by exploring the relationship between international donors and CSOs in trying to contribute to local peacebuilding in Libya. Libya has been challenging very hard governance situations owing to the absence of reconciliation between various rivals in the East and West regions, which have already imposed barriers on local human rights defenders and peacebuilders as Natil (2021) argues. This investigates important questions, including: To what extent have violence and militarism challenged CSOs' peacebuilders' and human rights defenders' lives, families, values, and commitments in Libya? What is the impact of protracted social and political conflict on CSOs' human rights defenders' local practices? How do local peacebuilders understand localism and local ownership in responding to violence and militarism? Has there been any differences between three regions in the East, West, and the South in Libya in responding to militarism and violence? However, the question of sustainability will remain a crucial issue for CSOs' local ownership and their peacebuilders and human rights defenders. For example CSOs have to persuade foreign donors while designing their programmes to be approved for funding.

Introducing and exploring these barriers facing local defenders and peacebuilders show how they have coped with these political and social shifts. This exploration has been done by revising the existing literature, individual experiences, and case studies while engaging with leaders, activists, and their CSOs to study the differences among the social contexts, cultural environments, and political dynamics to explore local practices. To enrich analyses by local experts, Ghazi Al-Assaf explores and introduces local response such as that of Jordanian CSOs including economic challenges imposed by civil war, which destroyed civil society and displaced hundreds of activists in a neighbouring country such as Syria. Al-Assaf highlights the issues of foreign aid and its impact on localism and policy changes, eradicating poverty. Al-Assaf reflected on these issues by presenting an evaluation of the effect of foreign aid on the civil society of Jordan in Chapter 7. Al-Assaf looks at the difficulties of how to effectively utilise the foreign aid and its impact on the local civil society organisations. The author looks at how, while foreign aid is intended to help, it can have a negative impact on civil society in the aid-receiving country by creating parallel structures of support or by diverting resources and individuals away from local attempts. This analysis seeks to capture many dimensions of the problems that foreign aid poses to the Jordanian economy and civil society. It will focus on the aspect of external assistance where sometimes despite the good intention of the donor, it may be counterproductive and may hamper sustainable development. Thus, analysing these challenges, it can be revealing the main issues of foreign aid policies and their impact on the local sustainable development of Jordan while responding to the immigrants' crisis post 2011, long Syria civil war.

Most of the contributions included in the edited volume are written by scholars from various locations. The volume provides the reader with empirically based, up-do-date, but still scientifically grounded analyses of local ownership and civil society responses to crisis in countries of the Cameroon, Poland, Egypt, Palestine, Libya, and Jordan, which can be appealing not only for an academic audience but also for international agencies, policymakers, and practitioners active in the region. It thus enriches the debate on the present and, especially, civil society in local ownership in the global south despite various political barriers, violence challenges, and militarism influence. The volume also assesses political contexts, social dynamics, and cultural dimensions along with CSOs' engagement with policymakers, donors, local stakeholders, and various partners. In other words, it attempts to present rigorous empirical research in a systematic way to explore a new concept and practices of local ownership by CSOs in adopting local and global challenges in the times of crisis.

References

Alexander, C. 2018. "The Soft Power of Development: Aid and Assistance as Public Diplomacy Activities." In *Handbook of Communication for Development and Social Change*, edited by J. Servaes. Singapore: Springer.

Asian Development Bank. 2009. *CSO Sourcebook: A Staff Guide to Cooperation with Civil Society Organizations*. Mandaluyong City. https://www.adb.org/sites/default/files/institutional-document/32629/cso-staff-guide_0.pdf

Bherer, L., P. Dufour, and F. Montambeault. 2016. "The Participatory Democracy Turn: An Introduction." *Journal of Civil Society* 12 (3): 225–30. https://doi.org/10.1080/17448689.2016.1216383.

Bojicic-Dzelilovic, V., and M. Martin. 2016. *Local Ownership Challenges in Peacebuilding and Conflict Prevention*. London School of Economics and Political Science.

Donais, T. 2012. *Peacebuilding and Local Ownership Post-Conflict Consensus-Building*. Routledge.

Natil, I. 2021. "Introducing Challenges to Youth Civic Engagement and Local Peacebuilding." In *Youth Civic Engagement and Local Peacebuilding in the Middle East and North Africa*, 1–12. Routledge.

Natil, I. 2022. *New Leadership of Civil Society Organisations: Community Development and Engagement*. London and New York: Routledge, Taylor and Francis Group.

Natil, I. 2023. *Public Diplomacy and Civil Society Organisations*. London and New York: Routledge, Taylor and Francis Group.

Natil, I., V. Malila, and Y. Sai, eds. 2020. *Barriers to Effective Civil Society Organisations: Political, Social and Financial Shifts*. Routledge.

Snow, N., and N. J. Cull. 2020. *Routledge Handbook of Public Diplomacy*. Routledge.

2 Local Humanitarianism and Organisational Complexities

Implementation of Safeguarding Measures

Sali Hafez and Ahmed El Assal

Introduction

Over the last decade, several Arab countries have been experiencing long-term political turmoil, civil wars, and ongoing conflicts. In 2021, Humanitarian Response Plans (HRPs) targeted seven countries, namely, Iraq, Libya, Palestine, Somalia, Sudan, Syria, and Yemen (UNOCHA 2021). Moreover, countries like Jordan, Egypt, and Lebanon hosted Syrian refugees amidst this regional complex displacement pattern (Ravesloot et al. 2022). Alongside this evolving reality, a remarkable surge in local humanitarianism has been observed, exemplified by establishing and expanding local humanitarian organisations, increased aid allocation for humanitarian action, and global focus on humanitarian actors' accountability for affected populations (Hilhorst et al. 2021; Schaaf et al. 2020). To ensure the accountability of the sector and the safeguarding of beneficiaries, several initiatives were launched to foster the Core Humanitarian Standards (CHSs) and strengthen safeguarding mainstreaming across the aid sector in the region.

Against this backdrop, this chapter directly engages with the main argument of this book and the scepticism that, in specific contexts, such as humanitarian settings and post-conflict countries, civil society organisations (CSOs) may lack the capacity to influence broader society. Yet, we argue that humanitarian organisations—as a sub-system of CSOs—may actively define and shape societal development and facilitate forming new ways of being held accountable to their communities and constituencies. Focusing on five Arab countries, Jordan, Lebanon, Yemen, Palestine, and Syria, undergoing humanitarian crises or conflicts, our analysis delves into the progress of local humanitarian organisations in safeguarding against Sexual Exploitation and Abuse (SEA)—a critical domain reshaping power dynamics and authority within the aid sector and recipient communities. This chapter attempts to fill a distinct gap in available data on practical lessons on organisational learning as it pertains to safeguarding. This is to say, there are not many examples of what works and what does not work for CSOs successfully implementing safeguarding mainstreaming across their policies, practices, and culture.

DOI: 10.4324/9781003565048-2

Using a mixed methods approach, this chapter explores how local humanitarian organisations have evolved in understanding, adopting, integrating, and implementing safeguarding measures in Arab countries. This chapter builds on a survey of 142 humanitarian organisations and focus group discussions with several organisations from the five countries to answer this question. In the context of the relatively new concept of safeguarding, often misconstrued with protection, local humanitarians redefine its parameters to address the emergent contractual dynamics among humanitarian actors, donors, and affected populations. This redefinition gains significance in the aftermath of sexual harassment incidents, triggering intertwined demands for bottom-up and top-down establishment of policies and procedures. Aligned with three key themes of the book—Local Ownership, International Actors and Donors, and CSOs in Humanitarian Crisis and War—our analysis contributes to a nuanced understanding of the intricate relationships and dynamics, shaping local responses to crises in the Arab region.

Following the introduction, this chapter is structured as follows: the next section presents a theoretical discussion of humanitarian actors' accountability frameworks, situating the concept of safeguarding within these theoretical debates. This chapter also presents the research methodology approach and data collection process. This is followed by a presentation of the key findings and results of the empirical research. We conclude with a discussion section and the implications of our findings on the state of safeguarding among civil society actors in the Arab region and beyond.

Humanitarian Organisations, Accountability, and Safeguarding

There has been growing attention and efforts from scholars and practitioners to hold development and humanitarian organisations accountable to their affected communities and populations (Seferis and Harvey 2022). For a long time, humanitarian organisations were guided by the humanitarian principles of impartiality, neutrality, and independence, with less emphasis on accountability and transparency practices (Hilhorst et al. 2021). Scholars have defined the accountability for CSOs as a relational concept between various stakeholders, including donors, governments, communities, and peer organisations (Ebrahim 2003). The focus on accountability practices, particularly safeguarding as a form of accountability of humanitarian actors, has become more dominant in academic and organisational discourses in recent years (Hilhorst, Bergh, and Chang Espino 2022), particularly when several scandals came to light in the humanitarian sector, among them the Oxfam GB women's sexual exploitation scandal in Haiti and the MeToo campaign of aid workers (Guardian 2018; Crack 2019).

Moreover, accountability theorists point out the rise of the accountability agenda in political and social debates over the last two decades (Gaventa,

Joshi, and Anderson 2023; Fox 2022). Lack of accountability among CSOs has also contributed to reduced funding, with people cancelling NGOs' subscriptions (Edwards 2018) or donors suspending aid to CSOs due to a lack of transparency and efficient safeguarding procedures (Crack 2019). Overall, efforts to foster accountability among development and humanitarian actors have taken different forms and built on different theoretical models.

Scholars have discussed "vertical accountability" or "upward accountability" to describe financial and legal accountability relationships between CSOs and their donors and governments (Ebrahim 2003; Crack 2019). In this form of accountability, CSOs, among other humanitarian actors, are required to report back to their donors (represented by foreign governments, philanthropy, or individual donations) through reporting and evaluation mechanisms (Hilhorst et al. 2021) or to their governments through established legal structures (Bloodgood, Tremblay-Boire, and Prakash 2013; Thrandardottir 2015). The increased dependency of CSOs on aid, mostly from northern government funding, has put them under scrutiny from donor agencies. Inspired by the New Public Management (NPM) agenda and the neoliberal policies in donor countries, CSOs were obliged to report on their spending of taxpayer money to donor agencies (Crack 2019). In recent years, donors have advocated for an increased demand for safeguarding policies—as a form of upward accountability—from both local and international organisations operating in development and humanitarian settings (Daoust and Dyvik 2020). However, the fragile state of law in humanitarian settings and the lack of government accountability in such settings limit the role of governments in investigating SEH complaints.

Another mechanism is "downward accountability", where organisations and humanitarian actors are foreseen to be held accountable by their programme beneficiaries, affected populations, and communities (Van Zyl and Claeyé 2019). This rhetoric emerged in the 1990s and became a major discourse among donors and CSOs. Its roots were embedded in people-centred development and human rights-based approaches (Crack 2019). The rationale behind downward accountability is that greater transparency and accountability of development and humanitarian actors to their communities will enhance the programming quality. It is also foreseen that the rights-based service delivery approach by local and international civil society actors should be strengthened. Overall, the shape and modalities of downward accountability may vary significantly, as Crack (2019) explains:

> Organisations have their own unique definitions of what they understand downward accountability to entail, but generally, these seem to converge on the following factors: (a) being answerable to communities for actions/inactions; (b) enabling communities to participate in decisions about NGO activities that potentially affect them; (c) enabling communities to have

> input in monitoring and evaluation processes; and (d) an obligation on NGOs to reflect on 'lessons learned' as a result of community interaction. (p. 624)

Several mechanisms are often referred to as part of the downward accountability approach, such as establishing community dialogue, complaint mechanisms, codes of conduct, and communication campaigns about the rights of the communities and the obligations of the organisations towards these communities. Most importantly, such mechanisms should be tailored to vulnerable and marginalised groups' needs and characteristics to empower them to speak and make their voices heard (Crack 2019; Holloway et al. 2020).

As a concept, Accountability to Affected People (AAP) gained traction in the humanitarian sector, putting the protection of beneficiaries at the centre of accountability relations—emphasising principles such as the do-no-harm approach (Seferis and Harvey 2022). Several initiatives, such as the Humanitarian Accountability Partnership (HAP), were established to set clear standards for accountability and quality management of humanitarian programmes following the AAP approach. Safeguarding of beneficiaries and programme participants has also become a key aspect of organisations' accountability to the affected population. It is often operationalised through complaints' mechanisms and safeguarding focal points in organisations. Overall, the literature shows that various concepts are used to describe these downward accountability relations between CSOs and programme beneficiaries, such as Communication and Community Engagement (CCE), Social Accountability (SA), Accountability to Affected Populations (AAP), and downward accountability. Another accountability strategy that emerged in recent years is "*internal accountability*". This mechanism refers to the organisation's ability to hold itself accountable to its internal constituency, including staff members, volunteers, the board of directors, and other internal stakeholders (Crack 2019). These efforts aim to enhance the working conditions of human resources related to the organisation, including paid staff and volunteers (Christensen and Ebrahim 2006).

To advance the accountability agenda in the development and humanitarian sector, several initiatives were launched to strengthen CSO accountability mechanisms, especially internal and downward accountability. For example, the Core Humanitarian Standards (CHS) Alliance, established in 2015, collates development and humanitarian organisations that use the CHS to advocate for people-centred aid. Nevertheless, CSOs have received significant criticism for their lack of ability to address several scandals of sexual misconduct and abuse for their staff members and beneficiaries of their programmes (Crack 2019). In recent years, there has been a surge in donors' emphasis on strengthening safeguarding policies in the development and humanitarian sector. Donors have demanded that their CSOs improve their safeguarding policies and procedures and increase the protection of "whistle-blowers" (Edwards 2018).

In this chapter, we adopt a definition of safeguarding as the mechanisms and practices that ensure that Prevention of Sexual Exploitation, Abuse and Harassment (PSEAH) measures are in place and establish adequate survivor-centred mechanisms to respond to an incident, properly handling cases, and safely carry out investigations. The forthcoming sections of this chapter examine safeguarding practices and policies as a form of accountability among CSOs across five Arab countries. This focus on safeguarding is well-suited to capture the dynamics of the different accountability loci outlined earlier. For instance, it reveals the close relationship between upward accountability practices and donor guidelines when developing safeguarding policies and commitments. Similarly, it sheds light on how community-based safeguarding efforts intersect with downward accountability to affected populations.

Methodology

This chapter reflects on key findings and discussions of a multi-country research study commissioned by the Safeguarding Resource Hub (SRH) and implemented by the authors along with two other research consultants. The study scope encompassed five countries in the region—Jordan, Lebanon, Syria, Yemen, and Palestine—selected for the study, based on existing safeguarding networks and collaborations supported by SRH. The research sought to understand experiences encountered by civil society organisations in the Arab states when implementing safeguarding policies and practices, considering challenges, and enabling factors in implementing their policies. Overall, the research aimed to answer the following research questions: What are the main challenges CSOs in the MENA region face regarding successfully implementing safeguarding across their procedures, practices, and organisational culture? How did some CSOs overcome such challenges? What motivates these organisations? What are the practical lessons that can be drawn from such successful examples? And what are some contextual differences between different countries in the MENA region about the successful implementation of safeguarding by CSOs?

Overall, the research team applied a mixed methods approach to answer these research questions, including several data collection activities between November 2022 and August 2023. First, the research team surveyed 142 organisations from the five countries. The survey was designed and carried out virtually using the Kobo Toolbox application in both Arabic and English. The purpose of the survey was to collect quantitative data on the status of safeguarding policies, organisational capacities, resources, and challenges CSOs face in implementing safeguarding measures across the region. The quantitative survey followed three regional focus group discussions, involving 20 CSOs of the surveyed organisations and in-depth conversations with five case studies from the aforementioned countries. Both methods aimed to unpack the experiences of organisations, particularly local CSOs, in establishing, implementing, and developing resources and capacities in safeguarding. This approach ensured representation from diverse stakeholders, including donors, the UN, INGOs, and CSOs within the MENA region. About 86 of these organisations were national organisations, while 56 were representatives from international organisations.

The data collected from the survey responses and interview recordings were analysed using a thematic analysis approach. Qualitative data underwent transcription and coding, allowing for the identification of common themes and patterns related to the research questions. The quantitative data from the survey were analysed using descriptive statistics to provide a regional overview of the state of safeguarding among the five surveyed countries. The analysis was triangulated across multiple data sources and validated with the SRH team in a sense-making workshop. The study centres the analysis on understanding safeguarding status, practices, challenges, and opportunities as indicative of accountability. By doing so, we actively ought to extract and analyse themes related to the wider humanitarian spaces and accountability from the interviews whenever encountered.

Despite the multiple strengths, the study exhibits a few limitations. First, the survey participation across the survey-participative countries was not representative. Lebanon showed low participation in comparison to other countries. Additionally, the study relied on qualitative data collected through interviews, which may be subject to biases or limitations in capturing the full range of perspectives and experiences. Findings are based on limited case studies and may not be fully generalisable to all contexts and organisations. The specific contextual factors and organisational characteristics discussed in this chapter may not be applicable or relevant to every safeguarding situation. Furthermore, the study did not evaluate the long-term impact and sustainability of the identified safeguarding practices. Future research should explore the impact and sustainability of these safeguarding practices.

The State of CSOs' Safeguarding in Syria, Yemen, Jordan, Lebanon, and Palestine

This section presents the key themes related to examining the state of safeguarding in the Arab states under study. The first theme explores the varying maturity and capacities of the study countries in safeguarding policies and practices. The second theme investigates the overall level of safeguarding and explores the prevalence of safeguarding policies, as well as the capacity of organisations to implement them effectively. The third theme examines the varying capacities and resources across countries and organisations. The fourth theme later examines the barriers to implementing safeguarding, focusing on the contextual barriers and how they differ from one country to another. Lastly, the fifth theme examines the drivers and enablers of implementing safeguarding policies.

Varying Maturity and Statuses

The focus on safeguarding in the Arab region is relatively recent, with varying degrees of experience and development across the countries of this study: Jordan, Lebanon, Syria, Yemen, and Palestine. Over the past five years, there has been a significant increase in the number of organisations that have adopted safeguarding policies in the development and humanitarian sector. Overall, the state of the safeguarding sector varies by country, where Jordan consistently scores high in terms of CSOs having a safeguarding policy in the humanitarian context. In contrast, we found relatively less development of safeguarding systems among CSOs in Yemen and Syria. This is understandable due to the nature of the aid structure, where many UN and donor agencies are based in Jordan and where there is a legacy of humanitarian work due to the longevity of the Palestinian refugee status in Jordan. Similarly, Lebanon demonstrates strong examples of safeguarding systems due to the vibrant civil society space and the existence of strong feminist and gender-focused CSOs. The research found that international and regional organisations have more financial and human resources to assign to safeguarding than local CSOs. The growth of safeguarding is donor-driven, prioritising project-specific rather than organisational-level safeguarding.

Increased Interest, Yet Inconsistent Enforcement

Findings from the survey suggest that the awareness of safeguarding at the institutional level across the sector is increasing and that there are some efforts to get policies in place; however, the enforcement of these policies is not yet consistent across organisations in the sector. Across the region, the enforcement of safeguarding policies remains patchy, with some organisations reporting that their policy is always enforced and others reporting that it is only sometimes enforced.

As revealed by the survey findings, 83% of the surveyed organisations (approx. 119 organisations out of 142 organisations) responded that they have a safeguarding policy in place, out of which 40 organisations developed their policy over the last 2–5 years and another 46 organisations developed their policy only in the previous 1–2 years. This surge in the number of organisations that decided to develop a safeguarding policy during this short period can be attributed to various efforts on both national and global scales. The research findings show an increasing focus from donors and international organisations over the past five years on supporting local actors to develop and strengthen their safeguarding systems.

The results show a variance across countries regarding the maturity of safeguarding policies. For instance many Jordanian organisations developed their safeguarding policy five years ago. Though only six organisations participated from Lebanon, 65% developed their policy over five years ago. In contrast, most organisations in Syria and Yemen developed safeguarding policies less than five years ago. This variation can be attributed to the level of maturity of the civil society sector whereby Jordan and Lebanon first started responding to the Syrian crisis. Furthermore, the capacity of CSOs to safeguard in active conflict countries has been more challenging.

When analysing the organisational responses by country on the extent to which organisational safeguarding policies are enforced, we found that approximately 30% of these organisations (39 organisations) responded that some policy procedures are enforced while others are not fully enforced. In comparison, 66% of the sample (90 organisations) responded that their safeguarding policy is fully enforced across all organisational areas. Only a small sample responded that the policy is not enforced.

Varying Capacities and Resources

The findings show that international and regional organisations have greater financial and human resources to support safeguarding efforts than CSOs. While most international and regional organisations (22 out of 28) responded that they have a dedicated resource person or focal point for monitoring the implementation of the safeguarding policy, this figure is significantly less among local and country-specific organisations. Almost 50% of the CSOs responded that they do not have a dedicated safeguarding point of contact or are unaware if this person exists. Participants emphasised the importance of having a dedicated resource person or focal point with clear roles and responsibilities to coordinate and support the implementation of the safeguarding policy and to work with the organisation management on their responsibilities to manage this, as well as with other stakeholders who need to meet the organisation's safeguarding requirements.

This is also reflected in the level of policy enforcement among local CSOs and international organisations. There is a significant variance between local and international organisations regarding their policy enforcement. The research shows that CSOs reported that some aspects of their safeguarding policy are not enforced, while this figure is less than that of international organisations.

Responses varied regarding the frequency of contact with the safeguarding focal point in each organisation. A figure of 30% of the respondents indicated that they meet regularly with their safeguarding focal points, while 70% of the responses showed that their interaction with the safeguarding focal point is limited to when they are designing a new programme or activity or when a complaint occurs. These findings imply that (a) organisations may still frequently respond to donor demands on individual programme requirements rather than considering safeguarding as a whole-organisation approach, and (b) there remains to be too much emphasis on reporting and response rather than on prevention. Safeguarding does not appear to be perceived as a preventive practice that requires constant interaction between staff and the person/focal point responsible for coordinating safeguarding implementation across the organisation's activities. No major variance was noticed for this observation across the different countries. Despite this, 93% of the organisations deliver training on safeguarding to their staff and volunteers, with different degrees of frequency.

The findings of the survey show that many organisations disseminate safeguarding materials and resources through multiple channels such as their websites, social media channels, flyers, and awareness-raising sessions in the communities. Still, 38% of the respondents are unaware if these materials exist within their organisation. Respondents suggested that organisations that receive funding for safeguarding should be sharing resources with less-resourced organisations that do not have the resources to develop or disseminate such material.

Management had an important role in implementing policies and procedures in most organisations. It is often the case that the implementation of policies is not efficiently monitored. The survey findings show that the management signs off on the policy and procedures but does not monitor their implementation or engage with safeguarding. For example management does not identify safeguarding risks to the organisation and puts mitigating measures in place. As outlined later in this chapter, organisational leadership is crucial to fostering a culture of transparency and accountability in safeguarding. To address this issue, further support is required by donors to hold organisational leaders to account to maximise their engagement and monitor safeguarding policies.

Barriers and Challenges

The main barriers encountered by CSOs are limited funding and resources to implement safeguarding such as financial resources to employ a dedicated safeguarding resource person, scarce allocation of personnel and resources to conduct safeguarding training, restricted overheads and, therefore, de-prioritisation of PSEA or safeguarding activities in donors funding, insufficient staffing, and limited or unavailable technical expertise with an in-depth understanding of the local contexts. Naik and Westendorf (2024) argue that addressing the root causes of sexual exploitation and abuse requires overcoming significant challenges. These include inadequate implementation of existing measures, insufficient political will to prioritise this issue, and a reluctance among donors and aid agencies to move beyond rhetoric and bureaucracy. Systemic and structural factors contribute to the prevalence of sexual exploitation and abuse, discouraging victims from reporting incidents and hindering effective investigations and accountability. Moreover, the irregular funding pattern for both PSEA and safeguarding and the sustainability and predictability of funding represented a barrier for local and national organisations compared to their international counterparts.

Another significant hurdle identified in the survey is the availability of technical guidance and tools in Arabic, as echoed by Elderfield and Kemp (2024). This challenge was predominantly reported by organisations in Yemen and Jordan and those operating regionally. The lack of Arabic and contextually appropriate resources can hinder CSOs' effective implementation of safeguarding policies and practices. During the FGDs, participants noted that some PSEA materials in Arabic were directly taken from other organisations or headquarters, and translations from English failed to encompass the countries' cultural sensitivity, social norms, legal frameworks, or penal codes. This observation was noted among both international and national CSOs.

The survey findings revealed that organisational leadership (including culture and structures) poses challenges in implementing safeguarding policies and practices, particularly in Yemen and Syria. As discussed in the scholarship of Gawn and Fraser (2024), there was a noted lack of emphasis on safeguarding as an institutional priority, resulting in inadequate attention and limited resources to implement any policy in place. Notably, no organisation in Lebanon reported this challenge, suggesting potential variations in organisational cultures and priorities across the MENA region, which can also be attributed to the low number of CSOs from Lebanon participating in the survey. Participants in the research expanded on this by recognising the role of leadership in enforcing safeguarding measures, without which it becomes a light-touch tokenistic exercise. Incidents of senior board members, showing limited familiarity with safeguarding or PSEA, delaying the adoption of, or not fully enforcing, policies, are reported most notably across Palestine, Yemen, and Syria.

This further highlighted the fragility of the legal systems and penal codes in countries like Yemen and Syria as additional barriers and challenges CSOs face in implementing safeguarding. These legal frameworks often fail to recognise or criminalise incidents that breach the organisational codes of conduct for safeguarding. This hampers prevention by ensuring staff understand that the conduct is inappropriate and responding by reporting serious harm and accessing survivor support. INGOs struggle to align international standards with organisational safeguarding policy, Standard Operating Procedures

(SOPs), and implementation with the national legal frameworks in the countries in which they operate.

INGOs expressed concerns regarding the centralisation of investigation mechanisms at the headquarters since this often implies lengthy investigation processes that can create challenges. This highlights the need for a nuanced approach considering each incident's specific context and circumstances. One significant finding is the misconception and confusion surrounding the term "safeguarding" among CSOs and affected communities. Safeguarding is a relatively new concept for many organisations in the sector, and it is often misunderstood and used interchangeably with PSEA and protection programme activities. Moreover, the impact of a high turnover rate among staff who lead safeguarding activities was reported as a challenge. This high turnover means routine activities such as awareness-raising, training, or case management are often inconsistent.

During the interviews, the challenge of deeply entrenched gender and social norms was highlighted. This exacerbates power imbalances, specifically in the humanitarian sector and the affected communities, leading to reluctance to report violations, as discussed by Javed, Chattu, and Allahverdipour (2021). The fear of retaliation and the potential negative impact on safety and access to services are significant deterrents to reporting incidents. Maintaining confidentiality and protecting the identity of reporting staff or community members emerge as a substantial challenge for many organisations.

Drivers and Enablers

The research showed several factors that supported the development and enforcement of safeguarding policies across the sector, which can be clustered into two main categories. The first set of enabling factors concerns the internal organisational structure and its leadership commitment to safeguarding. Participants in the survey from all participating countries emphasised the importance of organisational leadership in enforcing any organisational safeguarding efforts. Championing the safeguarding policy and creating a culture of accountability, which includes sanctions when the code of conduct is breached, signal to all staff members the organisation's commitment to safeguarding (Gawn and Fraser 2024).

An organisation's management or top leadership must ensure appropriate misconduct investigations. The management should also address misconceptions about complaints within an organisation by being clear that the lack of complaints does not mean that the organisation is performing well, but success is rather about applying adequate measures to respond to cases. To operationalise safeguarding, it is crucial to set adequate resource allocation and clear roles and responsibilities within the organisation. This includes having a dedicated safeguarding focal point within the organisational structure, which also means that all staff are aware of their responsibility for safeguarding and what that means for their work.

Participants also stated the need for donors and UN agencies to support humanitarian action, enforce safeguarding policies within their supported programmes, and guarantee that their implementing partners are held accountable and adhere to the policies they have in place. This should be a checklist and a part of the proposal submission requirements, as iterated by Cocking, Davies, and Finney (2022). The second set of factors addresses the external enabling environment where organisations with safeguarding policies work. As described, creating a safe and enabling environment for the complainant is crucial for reports to be made. This includes ensuring the confidentiality of complainants, survivors, and whistle-blowers. A "safe reporting" environment can be fostered through awareness-raising campaigns among programme participants to advocate rights and what constitutes abuse and mechanisms for reporting issues. Participants provided examples from their work, such as creating a hotline service for receiving complaints or a mobile application that can ensure the complainant's anonymity and indirect communication between the organisation and the complainant.

One of the Palestinian CSOs' successful examples is the SAWA "Together" Network, which operates through a hotline mechanism in the West Bank and Gaza. Based on the referral system, the network receives complaints from CSOs and UN agencies and investigates them safely and anonymously. Due to its impartiality in investigating complaints, the network has gained respect from the Palestinian humanitarian sector and is considered successful.

Discussion: Safeguarding Practices and Accountability Structures

This section explores the complex relationship between safeguarding practices and the accountability structures within the Arab world. It argues that the current approach to safeguarding, with its Western-centric origins and limited contextual understanding, poses significant challenges for enforcing local accountability. This section discusses five main themes: the first interrogates the origins and definitions of safeguarding and how it shaped its current understanding and enforcement in the Arab world. The second theme discusses the actors engaged in safeguarding and how they drive/discourage enforcing accountability. The third theme involves understanding the contextual particularities of safeguarding in the Arab world. The fourth theme examines how accountability is enforced, focusing on investigation pathways. Lastly, the fifth theme analyses how safeguarding practices are situated within the larger hierarchies, organisational structures, and social and gender norms.

First, the concept of safeguarding emerged in the wake of 2018, following the uncovering of sexual abuse scandals within multiple INGOs, which resulted in investigations and multiple policy processes such as the inquiry of the Commons Select Committee for International Development Committee (IDC) into sexual exploitation and abuse (Daoust and Dyvik 2022). As a result, Global-North-based humanitarian and development aid organisations made policy and funding commitments to safeguarding (Afrooz and Sloth-Nielsen 2020). Presented as a natural extension of the "Do No Harm" principle, safeguarding was initially conceptualised on the basis of the safeguarding definitions in the British legal system, particularly the British Charity Act—that all British INGOs adhere to (Daoust and Dyvik 2022). This definition and conceptualisation are deeply problematic—and arguably colonial—for the CSOs in the Arab world in two main ways.

First, its initial purpose prioritised accountability to Northern donor countries, such as the UK, with limited consideration of strengthening accountability mechanisms within recipient contexts (Daoust and Dyvik 2022). This one-sided focus overlooks the importance of investing in contextual-led definition and conceptualisation in the Arab states and how it can be enforced through sound and practical accountability mechanisms. Second, the definition of safeguarding mirrored the British legal framework, heavily weighted towards measuring individual vulnerabilities, framing vulnerabilities as apolitical characteristics, and focusing on key populations such as child protection or vulnerable adults (Daoust and Dyvik 2022). This narrow definition fails to capture the structural and systematic vulnerabilities of communities in humanitarian settings. The colonial roots of a modern concept are extremely alarming when presented in a humanitarian/development aid space that struggles to fight existing colonial structures and inherent power imbalances (Aloudat and Khan 2022). Consequently, safeguarding frameworks often fail to address these contexts' specific vulnerabilities and power dynamics. Furthermore, the imposition of Western-centric frameworks risks perpetuating the colonial structures and power imbalances that the humanitarian and development sector struggles to dismantle.

Second, the actors engaged in safeguarding drive/discourage enforcing safeguarding. The dominance of donors and INGOs in shaping safeguarding practices limits the prospects of accountability in Arab countries. Abimbola (2019) aptly describes the prevalence of a "foreign pose and gaze" among global actors, and we observed that most safeguarding technical experts, policy leads, and donors hold both foreign pose and gaze to humanitarian and development safeguarding in the Arab states. Our study found an appetite and interest from CSOs in enforcing and upscaling safeguarding within their organisations; however, the wider ecosystem is still underdeveloped, particularly in relation to engaging with the authorities, justice system, and the broader public system. This leads to a state of temporal interest that does not necessarily ensure sustainable development and interest.

The *third* theme examines the contextual specificity in the Arab world. While donors and international organisations have demonstrably increased their focus on supporting local actors in developing safeguarding systems over the past five years, these efforts suffer from a fundamental flaw: limited contextual conceptualisation of safeguarding in Arabic and among CSOs in the Arab world. This includes sensitivity to cultural norms, legal frameworks, and the specific vulnerabilities Arab communities face. This oversight hinders the establishment of functional downward accountability—a key principle for ensuring the safety and well-being of beneficiaries. A fundamental challenge lies in the translation of "safeguarding" in Arabic as "*al-soune*". The term itself lacks a precise translation, often conflated with the concept of "protection". The study participants' reliance on adapting INGO safeguarding policies or creating their own with limited local discussion underscores this lack of a shared understanding. This absence of a contextually relevant definition hinders the development of safeguarding practices and the appropriate accountability tools to achieve this. The shortcomings are further evident in the implementation gaps, particularly regarding the in-country legal system, which includes criminal laws, labour laws, and customs. However, as we observed in Northeast Syria and Yemen, the current approach often fails to consider these critical factors, especially in regions where state authorities are absent and alternative legal systems prevail. This disconnect raises concerns about the ability to implement safeguarding and risks the inability to respond to safeguarding concerns.

In a relevant line of the legal structures comes the *fourth* theme regarding the contextual accountability channels and mechanisms of safeguarding in Arab countries. Our understanding of the legal or alternative systems in which the CSOs operate is still incomplete, and the study captured diverse intra- and inter-geographic differences in how justice works. In Northeast Syria, where the Syrian regime's legal framework no longer applies, there is vagueness about the established justice system. Similarly, in Yemen, two legal systems are affiliated with the two authorities controlling different territories. We also observed instances, such as in Jordan, where the legal framework seemed more structured but did not include safeguarding violations in the penal/criminal code. The proposed solution of an international humanitarian ombudsman, championed by some INGOs, presents further contention. While intended as an alternative to self-regulation mechanisms, it remains unclear whether this proposal would include local actors and how it will be implemented (Carolei 2022). One limitation of our analysis is its limited focus on analysing the role of local authorities in facilitating/providing a barrier for enforcing safeguarding and establishing accountability—an area for future research. Moreover, there is very limited analysis and understanding of the role of traditional and tribal justice systems in enforcing safeguarding in the Arab states, especially in contexts where tribal or clan authorities are perceived to be powerful, such as in Jordan or Yemen.

Last, the *fifth* theme examines how the current safeguarding practices are situated within the larger hierarchies, organisational structures, and social and gender norms. We align with Daoust and Dyvik's (2022) argument on how safeguarding responses replicate familiar policies within the humanitarian and development sector and the persistence of interconnected gendered, racialised, and geographical power structures. This chapter highlights the multiple hierarchies where safeguarding is operating. At the organisational structures and leadership level, this chapter revealed how organisational leadership (including culture and structures) poses challenges in implementing safeguarding policies and practices, particularly in Yemen and Syria, while recognising that this was not a major challenge in Lebanon. Incidents of senior board members showing a limited familiarity with safeguarding or PSEA and delaying the adoption of, or not fully enforcing, policies are reported most notably across Palestine, Yemen, and Syria. Moreover, these organisational dynamics are nested in a wider social context where deeply entrenched gender inequality and gender-negative social norms discourage reporting, investigations, and accountability. In close interconnected communities, the concerns of maintaining confidentiality and protecting the survivor/reporter are deeply questioned. While safeguarding is reduced to a gendered depoliticised notion of protection against sexual exploitation and abuse, we observed a wide spectrum of analysis and depth in examining gender and social norms within the five countries. While gender was potentially weaponised and framed as a foreign colonial agenda in the context of Yemen, CSOs in Lebanon and Jordan showed a deeper understanding and analysis of this and examined it with a more nuanced understanding.

Conclusion

This chapter presents empirical evidence and initiates a discussion on the state of safeguarding in the Arab region, with an in-depth analysis of the process, drivers, enablers, and challenges of designing and implementing safeguarding policies and practices across five countries. Using a mixed methods approach, the chapter comprehensively presents how CSOs in the Arab countries designed, implemented, and mobilised resources in safeguarding, in addition to describing their journey in doing that. This chapter prioritised the voices of local CSOs and sought to understand the challenges and enabling factors they face. In addition, the study critically engages with theoretical and conceptual frameworks and investigates their appropriateness in the context of Arab countries. By providing in-depth contextual analysis, we examined how safeguarding relates to multiple institutional, legal, and social hierarchies in the examined countries, highlighting similarities and differences. Lastly, this study provided a bespoke analysis of the interaction between safeguarding and accountability.

Considering these findings, five main conclusionary remarks emerge from our research. First, contextualising safeguarding is crucial for efforts to foster safeguarding in the region. It is important to develop frameworks that are culturally sensitive and aligned with existing legal structures, including alternative systems. Second, local actors should be empowered as the main players in this arena. Thus, donors, among other actors, should prioritise local ownership by fostering collaboration and knowledge exchange between local and international actors. This ensures that safeguarding practices are responsive to the specific needs of the Arab communities. Third, strengthening the capacity of the humanitarian factor enhances the implementation and policymaking of safeguarding. This might entail providing targeted support to CSOs to enhance their capacity for resource mobilisation, policy development, and effective implementation of safeguarding measures. Finally, safeguarding should be rethought as a form of accountability. This should include exploring alternative accountability mechanisms that move beyond the current model focused on upward accountability to donors. Frameworks that prioritise downward accountability to beneficiaries can be more effective in the Arab context.

Acknowledgement

We would like to thank the MENA Safeguarding Resources Hub (SRH) for their continued technical backstopping during the conceptualisation and data collection phases of this research. We would also like to thank Ahmed Abd El Wahed and Mariia Kamianchyn for their roles during the writing of the extended report of this chapter and all the CSOs that contributed to the production of this study.

References

Abimbola, S. 2019. "The Foreign Gaze: Authorship in Academic Global Health." *BMJ Global Health* 4 (5): e002068.

Afrooz, K. J., and J. Sloth-Nielsen. 2020. "Safeguarding Children in the Developing World – Beyond Intra-Organisational Policy and Self-Regulation." *Social Sciences* 9 (6): 98.

Aloudat, T., and T. Khan. 2022. "Decolonising Humanitarianism or Humanitarian Aid?" *PLOS Global Public Health* 2 (4): e0000179.

Bloodgood, E., J. Tremblay-Boire, and A. Prakash. 2013. "National Styles of NGO Regulation." *Voluntas* 20 (10): 1–21.

Carolei, D. 2022. "An International Ombudsman to Make Non-Governmental Organisations More Accountable? Too Good to Be True." *Leiden Journal of International Law* 35 (4): 867–86.

Christensen, R. A., and A. Ebrahim. 2006. "How Does Accountability Affect Mission? The Case of a Nonprofit Serving Immigrants and Refugees." *Nonprofit Management and Leadership* 17 (2): 195–209.

Cocking, J., G. Davies, and N. Finney. 2022. *Independent Review of the Implementation of the IASC Protection Policy*. London: Oversees Development Institute (ODI).

Crack, A. 2019. "NGO Accountability." In *Handbook of NGOs and International Relations*, edited by T. Davies. London: Routledge.

Daoust, G., and S. L. Dyvik. 2020. "Knowing Safeguarding: The Geopolitics of Knowledge Production in the Humanitarian and Development Sector." *Geoforum* 112: 96–99.

Daoust, G., and S. L. Dyvik. 2022. "Reconceptualizing Vulnerability and Safeguarding in the Humanitarian and Development Sector." *Social Politics: International Studies in Gender, State & Society* 29 (1): 355–78.

Ebrahim, A. 2003. "Accountability in Practice: Mechanisms for NGOs." *World Development* 31 (5): 813–29.

Edwards, S. 2018. "Accountability in the Aid Sector: Humanitarians Can No Longer Be above the Law." Accessed April 18, 2024. https://www.devex.com/news/accountability-in-the-aid-sector-humanitarians-can-no-longer-be-above-the-law-92133

Elderfield, E., and E. Kemp. 2024. "We Don't Have a Word for That: Issues in Translating PSEA Communication." In *Sexual Exploitation and Abuse in Peacekeeping and Aid: Critiquing the Past, Plotting the Future*, edited by J. Westendorf and E. Dolan-Evans, 169–83. Bristol: Bristol University Press.

Fox, J. 2022. "Accountability Keywords." ARC Working Paper. Accountability Research Center, Washington, DC.

Gaventa, J., A. Joshi, and C. Anderson. 2023. "Citizen Action for Accountability in Challenging Contexts: What Have We Learned?" *Development Policy Review* 41 (1): 1–16.

Gawn, A., and E. Fraser. 2024. *Preventing SEAH in Aid Operation*. London: What Works to Prevent Violence Programme.

Guardian. 2018. "Timeline: Oxfam Sexual Exploitation Scandal in Haiti." Accessed April 20, 2024. https://www.theguardian.com/world/2018/jun/15/timeline-oxfam-sexual-exploitation-scandal-in-haiti

Hilhorst, D., S. Melis, R. Mena, and R. van Voorst. 2021. "Accountability in Humanitarian Action." *Refugee Survey Quarterly* 40 (4): 363–89.

Hilhorst, T., S. Bergh, and S. Chang Espino. 2022. "Closing the Accountability Gap: Community Perspectives and Experiences with Sexual Exploitation, Abuse, and Harassment (SEAH) in Occupied Palestinian Territories (oPt), Bangladesh, and Ethiopia." ISS Working Paper. International Institute of Social Studies (ISS), The Hague.

Holloway, K., V. Barbelet, A. Gray Meral, O. Lough, and A. Spencer. 2020. "Collective Approaches to Communication and Community Engagement: Models, Challenges, and Ways Forward." ODI Working Paper. Oversees Development Institute (ODI), London.

Javed, S., V. K. Chattu, and H. Allahverdipour. 2021. "Predators among Protectors: Overcoming Power Abuse during Humanitarian Crisis through Effective Humanitarian Diplomacy and a Gender-transformative Approach." *AIMS Public Health* 8 (2): 196–205.

Naik, A., and J. Westendorf. 2024. "Missing the Mark in PSEA." In *Sexual Exploitation and Abuse in Peacekeeping and Aid: Critiquing the Past, Plotting the Future*, edited by J. Westendorf and E. Dolan-Evans, 79–92. Bristol: Bristol University Press.

Ravesloot, B., T. Amirapu, M. Vallet, R. Alsalem, Y. Almustafa, C. Smith, C. Meisch, and L. Falk. 2022. *Regional Refugee and Resilience Plan Evaluation*. TANGO International Inc. Accessed May 3, 2024. https://www.3rpsyriacrisis.org/wp-content/uploads/2022/06/3RP_evaluation_June2022.pdf

Schaaf, M., V. Boydell, M. C. Sheff, C. Kay, F. Torabi, and R. Khosla. 2020. "Accountability Strategies for Sexual and Reproductive Health and Reproductive Rights in Humanitarian Settings: A Scoping Review." *Conflict and Health* 14 (1): 1–18.

Seferis, L., and P. Harvey. 2022. "Accountability in Crises: Connecting Evidence from Humanitarian and Social Protection Approaches to Social Assistance." BASIC Research Working Paper 13. Institute of Development Studies (IDS), Brighton.

Thrandardottir, E. 2015. "NGO Legitimacy: Four Models." *Representation* 51 (1): 107–23.

United Nations Office for the Coordination of Humanitarian Affairs – UNOCHA. 2021. "Global Humanitarian Overview: Part Two: Inter-agency Coordinated Appeals: Middle East and North Africa." Accessed May 3, 2024. https://2021.gho.unocha.org/inter-agency-appeals/middle-east-and-north-africa/

Van Zyl, H., and F. Claeyé. 2019. "Up and Down, and Inside Out: Where Do We Stand on NGO Accountability?" *The European Journal of Development Research* 31 (3): 604–19.

3 Humanity's Army

African Civil Society Organisations and the Protection of Civilians in Times of Crisis

Nguh Nwei Asanga Fon

Introduction

Since independence, Africa has been confronted with a myriad of challenges that undermine the well-being and welfare of its people. From armed conflicts, to natural disasters like drought, floods, famine, and pandemics, Africans have had their fair share of predicaments which are often exacerbated by mismanagement and dereliction of duty from government officials and government agencies (Edoun, Balgah, and Mbohwa 2015; Mahadevia 2021). State failures to manage the aforementioned type of crises usually result in humanitarian challenges like managing internally displaced persons and refugees during arm conflicts, providing relief for victims of natural disasters, and putting in place effective riposte measures against pandemics like COVID-19. All across Africa, civil society organizations (CSOs) are stepping up to the plate to respond to such challenges (Magiti 2005). For the most part, African CSOs are embedded and operate in local communities which endow them with proximity and empathy that are crucial in enhancing their ability to provide succour to those communities affected by humanitarian crises or challenges. This chapter explores the role CSOs in Sub-Saharan Africa have played in managing humanitarian crisis that emerged from armed conflicts. It specifically looks at empirical evidence of the strides made and challenges faced by these CSOs in managing the humanitarian challenges that accrued from the following crises: the terrorist activities of "Boko Haram" among countries of the Lake Chad Basin (Nigeria, Niger, Tchad, and Cameroon); the "Anglophone Crisis" in Cameroon; and the conflict in Central African Republic.

Historical and Contemporary Context of Humanitarian Crises in Africa

Humanitarian crises in Africa are driven by both natural and man-made factors. Armed conflicts have caused millions of deaths and economic losses in billions, destroying healthcare infrastructure and leaving behind landmines (Loretti and Tegegn 1997). Natural disasters, including epidemics,

DOI: 10.4324/9781003565048-3

droughts, and floods, disproportionately affect Africa, causing 60% of global disaster-related deaths despite only 20% of disasters occurring there (Ibid.). Climate change exacerbates these issues, impacting agriculture and food security (Buanango, Ferreira, and de Oliveira 2020). The combination of these factors, along with rapid population growth, poverty, and weak institutions, increases vulnerability to crises (Dunne and Mhone 2003).

The effectiveness of government responses to humanitarian crises in Africa has been mixed. While some improvements have been made, significant challenges remain. In the Sahel region, the 2012 food crisis response was larger and better than previous efforts but still fell short due to technical, financial, and political barriers preventing effective government leadership (Ford 2013a). Similarly, in Sudan and Somalia, humanitarian interventions have raised questions about the most appropriate ways to address complex emergencies (Prendergast 1997).

A civil society assessment of the Charter for Food Crisis Prevention and Management in the Sahel highlighted the need for improved governance and capacity building to enhance crisis management (Ford 2013b). Research across 17 sub-Saharan African countries found that effective governments with strong institutions, reliable law enforcement, and good infrastructure contribute to better food security for citizens (Sacks and Levi 2010). These findings underscore the importance of addressing systemic issues to improve humanitarian crisis responses in Africa.

Generally, African governments have faced criticism for their inadequate responses to humanitarian crises, often relying on external solutions that fail to address unique local challenges (Nyadera, Wandwkha, and Agwanda 2021). The failure of neoliberal policies and excessive government regulation have been blamed for exacerbating economic crises. Despite receiving trillions of dollars in foreign aid, African states continue to struggle with poverty, hunger, and disasters, partly due to corruption and poor economic management by leaders (Iwu 2022). The 2018–2020 Ebola outbreak in the Democratic Republic of Congo highlighted the importance of local involvement in crisis response. However, evidence suggests that international and national actors failed to adequately engage communities in decision-making or adapt to local concerns, maintaining a top-down approach (Mayhew et al. 2021). While immediate response methods have improved, including standardized needs' assessments (Campbell and Nair 2014), long-term solutions are needed. Experts argue for addressing root causes rather than just managing aftermath, emphasizing the need to tackle climate change, inequality, and resource conflicts to mitigate future crises (Ibid.).

To improve humanitarian responses, there is a need for transformation in international emergency systems, emphasizing inclusive collaboration with local actors and decentralizing decision-making power (Mayhew et al. 2021). One of the most important actors who can play a pivotal role to enhance the effectiveness of Africa's response to humanitarian crisis occurring on the continent are civil society organizations (CSOs). In the next section, we are going to look at the role of CSOs in humanitarian response from a general perspective.

The Role of Civil Society Organizations (CSOs) in Humanitarian Response

This section begins with a clear definition of what is meant by civil society organizations (CSOs), and what types of entities fit into this category. It also looks at the historical evolution of CSOs and their impact in Africa. Essia and Yearoo (2009) define civil society organizations (CSOs) as institutions that operate between the state, business, and family spheres. In terms of typology, CSOs encompass a wide range of entities, including NGOs, community-based organizations, trade unions, and professional associations. CSOs can be categorized into four main types: common cause, shared voice, research-oriented, and commercially oriented (Rainey, Wakunuma, and Stahl 2017). Their roles and prevalence vary across countries, influenced by the welfare state context and non-profit regime (Neumayr et al. 2009). According to DeMattee, CSOs are subject to regulatory regimes, which can be classified into four ideal types: rigid-conservatism, bureaucratic-illiberalism, permissionless-association, and legitimized-pluralism (DeMattee 2019). These regimes consist of laws and constitutional protections governing the civil society.

Historical Overview of CSOs and their Impact in Africa

Civil society organizations (CSOs) in Africa have experienced significant growth and evolution over the past few decades. Their role expanded dramatically in the 1990s, coinciding with the HIV/AIDS crisis and socio-economic challenges (Wamai 2013). CSOs, including NGOs and community-based organizations, have been crucial in addressing health issues, particularly HIV/AIDS, by implementing programs, developing policies, and channelling funds to affected populations. In this light, Wamai (2013) underscores that CSOs have been instrumental in addressing the HIV/AIDS crisis, reducing incidence by 25% in 22 African countries and expanding treatment access.

In West Africa, CSOs have contributed to promoting human rights, preventing mass atrocities, and protecting civilians in conflict-affected areas (Eze 2016). CSOs, including domestic and international organizations, have been actively involved in managing refugee crises in the Middle East and North Africa regions (Fisseha 2018). CSOs have also played a vital role in social mobilization, helping families access healthcare services and overcome barriers to care. However, CSOs face challenges such as dependency on donor funding, which may compromise their autonomy and performance

(Chaplowe and Engo-Tjega 2007). Recently, the COVID-19 pandemic has further impacted African CSOs, necessitating adaptations in their operations and responses (Eribo 2021). Despite these challenges, CSOs continue to be essential actors in Africa's development landscape, particularly in health and social sectors. CSOs operating in Africa CSOs have demonstrated their capacity to complement government efforts in peace and security, leveraging their in-depth knowledge of local contexts and expertise in working closely with communities (Eze 2016).

Humanitarian Impact of the Armed Conflicts: Boko Haram Case

This section provides an overview of the humanitarian impact of three particular conflicts that constitute part of our case study selection: the terrorist activities of Boko Haram in the Lake Chad Basin, the Anglophone Crisis in Cameroon, and the conflict in the Central African Republic (CAR). The Boko Haram insurgency in the Lake Chad Basin has resulted in a severe humanitarian crisis, with over 20,000 people killed and millions displaced (Awosusi 2017). The violence has devastated infrastructure, disrupted livelihoods, and created food insecurity for millions (Idika-Kalu 2020). The region faces significant health challenges, with half a million children at risk of severe acute malnutrition and limited access to healthcare facilities (Awosusi 2017). Socio-economic impacts include reduced trade, increased poverty, and dependence on aid (Idika-Kalu 2020). In Nigeria, which is one of the countries most severely affected by the crisis, the Boko Haram insurgency has had severe humanitarian consequences, resulting in numerous casualties, human rights abuses, and population displacement (Okoli and Iortyer 2014). It has also led to food insecurity, collapse of small businesses, and increased poverty levels in affected regions (Illo, Akanmu, and Osman 2023).

Generally, the Boko Haram insurgency has significantly impacted human security, threatening access to education, healthcare, and livelihoods. It has caused widespread destruction of infrastructure, including houses, schools, and healthcare centres, forcing many to live in constant fear (Amalu 2015). In Nigeria, the Boko Haram insurgency has resulted in severe humanitarian consequences, including thousands of deaths, millions of displaced persons, and widespread trauma (Ehwarieme and Umukoro 2015; Abdulmalik et al. 2019)

The crisis has also led to a rise in internally displaced persons and refugee situations. Studies have found a significant relationship between Boko Haram's activities and humanitarian crises, particularly in terms of human casualties, food insecurity, and internal displacement (Emmanuelar 2015). Addressing issues of poverty, corruption, and governance is crucial for effective counter-insurgency efforts and improving human security in Nigeria.

The Humanitarian Impact of the Anglophone Crisis in Cameroon

The Anglophone crisis in Cameroon, which began in 2016, has led to a complex humanitarian emergency characterized by massive forced displacement (Samah and Tata 2021). Internally displaced persons face challenges straddled between government forces and armed separatists, with inadequate state protection and assistance (Ibid.). The crisis has severely impacted Cameroon's economy, society, and diplomacy, leading to significant socio-economic challenges for local communities (Ollong 2021; Sayem 2020). Humanitarian actors have become more involved, but their efforts are hindered by a reliance on government subsidies and lack of coordination (Muntoh 2020). Women and children have been particularly affected, facing untold misery (Ashu 2020). In a special report on the conflict dedicated to women issued in February 2022, International Crisis Group (ICG) presented a map that highlights the ordeal encountered by women and children in both regions involved in the conflict.

Despite the involvement of humanitarian actors, their efforts have been limited due to reliance on government subsidies and international aid (Muntoh 2020). The conflict has exposed Cameroon's inadequacies in protecting and assisting its forcibly displaced populations (Samah and Tata 2021).

The Humanitarian Impact of the Conflict in Central African Republic

The conflict in the Central African Republic (CAR) has had severe humanitarian consequences. The crisis, which began in 2013, has led to the displacement of approximately 25% of the population (Schneider and Ferguson 2020). The conflict has also led to widespread human rights violations and near-genocidal violence between Muslims and Christians (Kane 2014). Despite international peacekeeping efforts, the situation remains critical, with the United Nations describing it as an alarming security threat (Schneider and Ferguson 2020). Recent mortality surveys have uncovered an alarming health emergency in CAR, with a crude mortality rate of 1.57 deaths per 10,000 people per day, which is four times higher than UN statistics suggest (Gang, O'Keeffe, and Roberts 2023). The study also found that malaria/fever and diarrhoea were the primary reported causes of death, with violence accounting for 6% of all deaths. These findings underscore the urgent need for increased humanitarian assistance, particularly in rural areas outside the government control (Gang, O'Keeffe, and Roberts 2023).

The international community's approach has been largely reactive and ineffective, focusing on stabilization rather than addressing the root causes of violence and governance issues (Abdullahi 2020). The conflict has also exposed significant challenges in documenting health and humanitarian needs in CAR, with official statistics dramatically underestimating birth and death rates in conflict settings (Kuehne and Roberts 2021).

CSOs' Response to Selected Humanitarian Crises in Africa

Given the failure of governments and the international community to fully manage the humanitarian consequences of conflicts in Africa, CSOs have been stepping up to the plate to complement the efforts of the former. In this section, we are going to examine the role played by African CSOs to address the humanitarian impact of the Boko Haram terrorist activities in the lake Chad Basin, the conflict in the Anglophone regions of Cameroon, and the civil war that took place in the Central African Republic.

CSOs' Response to the Boko Haram Terrorist Activities in the Lake Chad Basin

In order to have a more detailed and specific analysis of the situation, and given the fact that Nigeria constitutes one of the countries that have been most severely hit by the Boko Haram insurgency, I have decided to narrow my focus on the activities of Nigerian CSOs. Local civil society organizations and NGOs in Nigeria have responded to the humanitarian challenges posed by Boko Haram's activities with mixed results. While NGO activities are generally positive, smaller NGOs adhering to classical humanitarian aid models may inadvertently prolong the conflict (Adeakin, Gray, and Madu 2021). Abdulmalik et al. 2019) underscore that local civil society organizations in Nigeria have played a significant role in addressing these issues, though their efforts were initially hampered by poor coordination and security challenges. The authors add that innovative responses have emerged, such as task-sharing approaches to mental health support and collaboration with development partners (Abdulmalik et al. 2019).

The crisis has led to widespread displacement, food insecurity, and malnutrition, particularly affecting women and children. NGO responses have been hindered by uncoordinated efforts and government inefficiency, with corruption identified as a major obstacle. Some humanitarian support has had adverse effects, including increased domestic violence, social cohesion disruption, and sexual exploitation (Abdullahi and Chikaji 2020). Additionally, NGOs have faced accusations of supporting Boko Haram (Ibid.). To address these issues, recommendations include stricter regulation of NGO operations, increased focus on capacity-building programmes, and improved coordination among stakeholders (Abdullahi and Chikaji 2020).

Challenges Faced by Nigerian CSOs

Nigerian CSOs have faced numerous challenges in addressing the humanitarian crisis caused by Boko Haram in Nigeria. These include security risks, limited resources, and coordination difficulties (Adeakin, Gray, and Madu 2021). Local CSOs struggle with the classical model of humanitarian aid, which may inadvertently prolong the conflict (Adeakin, Gray, and Madu 2021). Matters have been made worse by the Nigerian government's inadequate response to the humanitarian effects of the crisis with corruption hindering the effective coordination of relief efforts.

Women and Youth Empowerment Integration

One of the organizations leading the charge in addressing the humanitarian challenges caused by the terrorist activities of Boko Haram in Nigeria is the Integrated Women and Youth Empowerment Centre (IWAYEC). IWAYEC is a community-based CSO with headquarters in Maiduguri, Borno State, which happens to be the birthplace of Boko Haram and epicentre of the Boko Haram terrorism. IWAYEC focuses on the empowerment of women, youth, and vulnerable populations through education, skills development, and psychosocial support. Its mission is to create opportunities for individuals, especially those in conflict-affected areas like the Lake Chad Basin, to rebuild their lives and contribute to their communities. Its activities include providing the provision of quality education to displaced and conflict-affected children and youth through initiatives such as the Education in Emergencies (EiE) programme and the Girls in STEM (Fon 2024).

IWAYEC has been working in areas in Nigeria affected by the Boko Haram crisis for the past 20 years. Its Executive Director, Afiniki Mangzha, had the following to say about her organization's response and achievements vis-à-vis the humanitarian crisis caused by Boko Haram in Nigeria:

> IWAYEC has been at the forefront of responding to the humanitarian crisis in the Lake Chad Basin, especially in Borno State. We have focused on education, psychosocial support, and livelihood interventions for internally displaced persons (IDPs), particularly women, children, and youth. We've implemented projects like the Education in Emergencies (EiE) program, Girls in STEM, and the Digital Mobile Library for IDP camps. These initiatives aim to restore a sense of normalcy, provide education, and empower victims to rebuild their lives.
>
> One of our most successful initiatives is the EiE program, which we implemented in partnership with UNICEF across 17 schools in Borno State. This program has provided educational opportunities to thousands of children who would otherwise have been deprived of learning due to the

> conflict. Additionally, our Girls in STEM project has empowered young girls with the skills and confidence to pursue careers in science and technology, breaking the cycle of poverty and dependence. One success story is that of a young girl from Borno who participated in our Girls in STEM program. Despite losing her family to Boko Haram, she excelled in her studies and is now pursuing a degree in engineering, determined to rebuild her community.
>
> (Fon 2024)

One of the keys to the success of IWAYEC in its efforts to handle the humanitarian challenges from the Boko Haram crisis is coordination and collaboration with other stakeholders. To this end, Ms Mangzha underscored that IWAYEC works coordinating with the local authorities, other CSOs, and international partners in ensuring a harmonized approach in the delivery of humanitarian assistance. She specifically cited collaboration with the following stakeholders in the implementation of some their projects: Nigeria's Ministry of Women Affairs and Social Development and the United Nations Infant Emergency Fund (UNICEF) (Ibid.). In practical terms, this collaboration includes joint planning sessions, regular meetings, and shared monitoring and evaluation frameworks to avoid duplication and ensure complementation. Concerning the challenges faced by IWAYEC in the provision of humanitarian assistance to victims of Boko Haram activities, Mangzha pointed out the following:

> The challenges are multifaceted. First, the security situation is volatile, making access to certain areas difficult and dangerous. Second, there's a lack of sufficient funding to meet the growing needs of the affected population. Third, there are logistical challenges, such as poor infrastructure and communication networks, which hinder the delivery of aid. Lastly, there's the psychological trauma experienced by the victims, which complicates the process of reintegration and recovery.
>
> (Fon 2024)

One of the key challenges with humanitarian workers engaged in conflict zone has always been security. This is equally a crucial concern for IWAYEC, which has taken concrete measures to secure their staff who are working in zones affected by Boko Haram insurgency. These measures include training on measures of security and safety, the enforcement of strict security protocols including security briefings, the use of secure communication channels, and regular risk assessment; collaboration with local authorities and security officials; and the putting in place of contingency plans for staff evacuation in case of the deterioration of the security situation.

CSOs' Humanitarian Response to the Anglophone Crisis in Cameroon

Cameroonian CSOs have played a crucial role in addressing humanitarian issues arising from the Anglophone crisis in Cameroon. It is important to mention that in addition to formally registered CSOs, the response in this section encompasses the activities of informal groupings like local women and local communities in general. CSOs have focused on protecting human rights, promoting social justice, and advocating for gender equality (Moinina and Ngoh 2020). They have engaged with affected communities, documented the conflict's impact on civilians, and drawn national and international attention to the crisis (Annan et al. 2021). One of the areas where CSOs have been very active is that of providing humanitarian assistance to victims of the crisis like internally displaced persons. In this regard worth citing are the actions of Higher Glory Society (HIGLOS) and Community Initiative for Sustainable Development (COMINSUD), both located in the North West Region of Cameroon, which provide material and non-material assistance to the victims of the conflict (Engwari and Njiei 2021). Local CSOs have also maintained pressure for a negotiated settlement through public protests and interactions with both government and non-state armed groups. However, their efforts have been hampered by shrinking civic space and intimidation (Annan et al. 2021).

Local Humanitarian Response to the Anglophone Crisis in Cameroon

Local communities have also initiated indigenous conflict resolution mechanisms, though their effectiveness is limited by various factors. Within this framework, it is important to highlight the activities of local women in tackling the humanitarian crisis, given the pivotal but often neglected role women play in arm conflict. The International Crisis Group (ICG) has produced a special report that reveals the contribution of Cameroonian women in addressing the humanitarian impact of the Anglophone crisis. Talking about the aforementioned issue, ICG underscores the following:

> Cameroonian women also engage widely in peacebuilding activities. These activities are far from monolithic. Urban, high-profile women's groups easily engage with national and international institutions, while rural grassroots activists have more sway over separatist fighters but few connections with officials in Yaoundé. . . . Although the government and separatists often disregard women's activism or relegate activists to narrow, single-issue politics, women, both at home and abroad, have pressed with some success for relief measures such as reopening schools that separatist boycotts forced to close and extending the reach of humanitarian

> aid. They have also called for broader peace initiatives, like ceasefires and inclusive talks. As women's activism has become bolder and more prominent, the government has become less tolerant of it, and activists also face reprisals by separatists in areas where they operate.
>
> (International Crisis Group 2022)

It should be noted that the crisis has led to massive forced displacement, with internally displaced persons (IDPs) caught between government forces and armed separatists (Samah and Tata 2021). Despite these challenges, CSOs have adapted and resisted restrictions, demonstrating resilience in their humanitarian efforts (Annan et al. 2021).

Challenges Faced by CSOs in Anglophone Crisis

In terms of challenges, it is worth mentioning that local CSOs working in the area have faced significant impediments to their efforts to address the humanitarian problems emanating from the crisis. Prominent among these challenges are restrictions from the government. Annan et al (2021) underscore that CSOs face a shrinking civic space, with restrictions on their activities and intimidation from authorities. Despite these constraints, CSOs have contributed to conflict resolution by engaging affected communities, raising awareness, and advocating for negotiated settlements. Among the CSOs making significant strides in tackling the humanitarian challenges caused by the ongoing conflict in the Anglophone regions in Cameroon is Higher Glory Society (HIGLOS).

The organization saw the light of day in 2013 as an initiative to reach out to young girls within the community and provide them with resources and opportunities to maximize their potentials. The mission of HIGLOS is to contribute to bringing less privileged women and girls to higher state of triumph by enhancing their economic empowerment through agriculture and vocational training. It started operations in the conflict-ridden North West region in 2020 with a focus on providing humanitarian assistance to victims of the conflict, especially IDPs. Talking about the contribution made by HIGLOS to address the humanitarian challenges caused by the ongoing conflict in the Anglophone regions of Cameroon, its Project Manager Mr John Tiyang underscored the following:

> HIGLOS has provided non-food items to victims consisting of vocational training to teenage female victims as well as provided the tools for their social reinsertion. A specific example I can cite is that of a victim teenage mother we trained in tailoring. Upon providing all the equipment and materials she needed to start her own tailoring workshop, she is now an independent proud wealth creator.
>
> (Fon 2024)

Concerning the challenges faced by HIGLOS in providing humanitarian assistance to the victims of the Anglophone crisis, Tiyang identified limited financial resources as their main difficulty. When it comes to coordination with other CSOs, local authorities, and international organizations in addressing the needs of civilian victims of the crisis, Tiyang pointed out that this is done through project collaboration in which his organization conceives humanitarian projects, solicits, and receives funding for their execution from international organizations (Fon 2024). Concerning security measures, Tiyang admitted that HIGLOS is yet to develop a protocol for the safety and security and safety of its workers, one of whom was attacked on her way to deliver support to victims of the crisis.

CSOs' Response to the Conflict in Central African Republic

Civil society organizations in the Central African Republic (CAR) have played a crucial role in addressing humanitarian challenges caused by the civil war. Local NGOs were instrumental in instigating the International Criminal Court's involvement in CAR, creating a receptive environment for justice initiatives (Glasius 2009). An inter-religious humanitarian response emerged, with Muslim agencies partnering with Christian organizations to provide aid and promote conflict-sensitive solutions (Mahony 2014). These efforts have been part of a broader strategy to protect vulnerable groups, including forcibly displaced populations and victims of armed conflict (Samah 2021; Glasius 2009). The most impressive contribution of CSOs in the addressing the humanitarian effects of the conflict in CAR has come from inter-religious entities and initiatives like the Inter-Religious Platform in CAR comprising Christian and Muslim religious officials. Catherine Mahony of the Catholic Agency for Overseas Development (CAFOD) has written a poignant report on inter-religious humanitarian response to the conflict in the CAR in which she underlined the following, concerning the work of the Inter-Religious Platform (officially known as La Platforme des Confessions Religieuses en Centrafrique) in the country:

> The Inter-Religious Platform, comprising Archbishop Dieudonné Nzapalainga, Imam Omar Kobine Layama and Pastor Nicholas Guérékoyame Gbangou, has continuously worked to communicate a message of moderation, tolerance and respect through dialogue with communities but also by example in their own actions. As tensions and violence between communities increased, the Archbishop and the Imam decided to live together at the Archbishop's home, to offer protection to each other and to set an example of peace and cohesion despite the ongoing conflict. The efforts of the Inter-Religious Platform have also been instrumental in drawing international attention to the crisis in CAR.
>
> (Mahony 2024)

Furthermore, local faith communities have contributed material and non-material resources to crisis-affected populations, although their involvement presents both opportunities and challenges for humanitarian organizations (Ager, Fiddian-Qasmiyeh, and Ager 2015).

Challenges Faced by CSOs in the CAR

Local civil society organizations (CSOs) in the Central African Republic (CAR) face numerous challenges in addressing humanitarian issues stemming from ongoing conflicts. Insecurity is the primary risk, necessitating a multidimensional approach that includes gaining acceptance from local communities and conflict parties (Malhouni and Mabrouki 2024). Local CSOs in CAR also struggle with logistical obstacles, procurement issues, and technical risks, particularly during initial deployment phases (Malhouni and Mabrouki 2024). While local CSOs have played a crucial role in instigating the International Criminal Court's involvement in CAR, they face long-term challenges such as slow-paced investigations, inadequate outreach, and limited capacity to provide physical and material security to victims (Glasius 2009). Additionally, the blurred lines between state and society, and between "civil" and "uncivil" actors in fragile contexts, complicate efforts to strengthen the civil society in support of peace (Verkoren and van Leeuwen 2014). Local CSOs are already playing a significant role in addressing the humanitarian challenges posed by the conflict in the Central African Republic, but their performance can be better if helped.

Inter-Religious Intervention

The Inter-Religious Platform, officially known as *La Plateforme des Confessions Religieuses en Centrafrique* (PCRC), is an important civil society coalition in the Central African Republic (CAR) that brings together leaders from the Christian, Muslim, and Protestant communities. Established in 2013 during the height of the civil war in CAR, the platform was formed in response to the escalating violence and sectarian conflict that had deeply divided the country along religious lines (KAICIID 2024). The PCRC's primary mission is to promote peace, dialogue, and reconciliation among the different religious communities in CAR. It was co-founded by three prominent religious leaders: Imam Omar Kobine Layama, representing the Muslim community; Reverend Nicolas Guérékoyame-Gbangou, representing the Evangelical Church; and Cardinal Dieudonné Nzapalainga, representing the Catholic Church (Newey 2024).

In addition to its peacebuilding efforts, the PCRC has played a crucial role in providing humanitarian relief to victims of the civil war. The conflict, which has displaced hundreds of thousands of people and resulted in severe humanitarian crises, has left many in desperate need of food, shelter, medical care, and psychological support. The PCRC has collaborated with international organizations, NGOs, and local communities to facilitate the delivery of aid to those affected by the conflict, regardless of their religious affiliation. The platform has been instrumental in organizing and coordinating efforts to distribute food and non-food items to displaced populations, setting up temporary shelters, and providing medical assistance in areas where the conflict has disrupted normal health services. Furthermore, the PCRC has advocated for the protection of civilians and the respect of human rights (Newey 2024), working to ensure that aid reaches the most vulnerable populations.

The work of the PCRC has been widely recognized both within CAR and internationally as a model of interfaith cooperation in conflict zones. Despite the challenges posed by ongoing violence and instability, the platform continues to be a beacon of hope for many in CAR, demonstrating that religious leaders can play a vital role in fostering peace and delivering humanitarian aid in times of crisis. However, the PCRC faces ongoing challenges, including limited resources, security threats, and the complex dynamics of the conflict. Despite these hurdles, the platform remains committed to its mission of peace and humanitarian support, striving to build a more stable and united Central African Republic.

Comparative Analysis of CSO Response to the Humanitarian Crisis

African civil society organizations (CSOs) have played pivotal roles in responding to humanitarian crises in various sub-regions, often stepping in where government and international efforts have fallen short. However, the nature, effectiveness, and challenges of these responses vary significantly across different contexts, as seen in the cases of the Boko Haram insurgency in the Lake Chad Basin, the Anglophone crisis in Cameroon, and the civil war in the Central African Republic (CAR). This variation can be seen from the following angles: scope and focus of responses, coordination and collaboration, challenges faced, and impact and effectiveness.

Scope and Focus of CSO Responses

There has been a significant difference in the area of focus and scope of humanitarian actions undertaken by CSOs in their response to the various crises considered in this chapter. Concerning addressing the humanitarian challenges caused by the terrorist activities of Boko Haram Crisis in Nigeria, Nigerian CSOs have concentrated their efforts on addressing immediate humanitarian needs like displacement, food insecurity, and mental health. They have also faced accusations of inadvertently prolonging the conflict by adhering to classical humanitarian models that may not be well-suited to the complexities of the crisis.

Meanwhile, Cameroonian CSOs have taken a broader approach in addressing the humanitarian impact of the conflict in the Anglophone regions of Cameroon. Their attention and efforts have focused on human rights protection, social justice, and gender equality. Women's groups, in particular, have played a crucial role in peacebuilding and advocacy, despite facing repression from both the government and separatists. As concerns the civil war in CAR, Central African CSOs have been instrumental in mediation and inter-religious dialogue, particularly through the Inter-Religious Platform, which has promoted peace and tolerance amidst the conflict. These organisations have also been pivotal in engaging international mechanisms, such as the International Criminal Court (ICC), to address issues of justice.

Coordination and Collaboration

There has also been some disparity when it comes to coordination and collaboration of various stakeholders involved in the management of the three humanitarian crises analysed in this chapter. Concerning the Boko Haram terrorist activities in the Lake Chad Basin, the response in Nigeria has been marked by poor coordination among CSOs, government bodies, and international actors. This lack of coordination has been a significant obstacle, exacerbated by government inefficiency and corruption.

As concerns the conflict in the Anglophone regions of Cameroon, there has been some synergy among CSOs involved in addressing the humanitarian impact of the conflict. Despite facing restrictions, Cameroonian CSOs have managed to maintain some level of coordination, particularly in advocating for negotiated settlements. However, their efforts are often hampered by a shrinking civic space and government intimidation. The most eloquent demonstration of synergy among CSOs has come from the CAR where those involved in addressing the humanitarian impact of the civil war have shown strong collaboration, particularly through inter-religious initiatives. The Inter-Religious Platform exemplifies how collaboration across religious lines can be a powerful tool for peacebuilding and humanitarian assistance, despite the complex and fragile environment.

Challenges Faced by CSOs

In terms of challenges, the experiences on the field demonstrate some similarities and few differences. CSOs in all the three conflict areas (Nigeria, Cameroon, and the CAR) are all confronted with security risks and logistical deficiencies. Unique challenges faced by African CSOs include: the unintended consequences of traditional humanitarian models, as well as bureaucratic corruption and inefficiency for Nigerian CSOs; government-imposed restrictions, a shrinking civic space for Cameroonian CSOs; and in the case of the CAR, the complex dynamics of operating in a fragile state where the lines between civil and uncivil actors are often blurred.

Impact and Effectiveness

The impact and effectiveness of CSOs involved in addressing the humanitarian challenges caused by the conflicts analysed in this chapter also vary. While Nigerian CSOs have had some success in addressing the immediate humanitarian needs, their overall impact has been limited by systemic issues such as poor coordination and government inefficiency. The potential for these efforts to inadvertently prolong the conflict is a significant concern. By contrast, CSOs in Cameroon and CAR have been more effective and had more profound impact in managing the humanitarian challenges resulting from the conflicts in the respective countries. Concerning the conflict in the Anglophone regions of Cameroon, the impact of Cameroonian CSOs has been significant in terms of raising awareness and advocating for human rights, all these despite facing considerable opposition. Their involvement in peacebuilding, particularly through women's activism, has been a notable success, though it remains under threat from ongoing repression.

Similarly, the impact of CSOs in addressing the humanitarian challenges caused by the civil war in the CAR, especially through inter-religious initiatives, has been profound. Central African CSOs have been very effective in promoting peace and tolerance. Their ability to engage international mechanisms for justice also highlights their effectiveness in addressing the broader implications of the conflict.

Enhancement Effectiveness of African CSOs

It is evident from the aforementioned case study analysis (Boko Haram insurgency in Nigeria, the Anglophone conflict in Cameroon, and the war in Central African Republic) that African CSOs play a crucial role in addressing the humanitarian challenges posed by conflicts on the continent albeit the multifarious difficulties they are confronted with on the field. This chapter added first-hand accounts on the activities of CSOs by sharing responses to interviews carried out with actors on the field. It will also be important to share the perspectives of the field actors (representatives of CSOs on the frontline in Cameroon and Nigeria) on lessons to be learnt from current crisis and recommendations on how to enhance the work of CSOs in times of crisis.

Lessons from Past Crisis

It is often said that those who fail to learn from history are bound to repeat the same mistakes. It is therefore important to draw some lessons from the humanitarian engagement of African CSOs in conflicts on the continent. Here are the views of IWAYEC's Executive Director, Afiniki Mangzha, and HIGLOS Project manager John Tiyang on the issue. Mangzha presents us with three lessons that the international community can draw from the humanitarian challenges caused by the Boko Haram insurgency:

> One key lesson is the importance of community engagement. Involving the affected communities in the planning and implementation of projects ensures that the interventions are culturally appropriate and sustainable. Another lesson is the need for flexibility and adaptability. The situation on the ground can change rapidly, and our response must be able to adjust to these changes. Lastly, building strong partnerships with local and international stakeholders enhances the effectiveness and reach of our interventions.
>
> (Fon 2024)

Based on the poor implementation of some CSO-sponsored projects by grant beneficiaries, Tiyang had the following to say concerning what can be done to boost the productivity, profitability, and sustainability of projects run by victims of conflict who benefit from such funding: "Victims must be made to contribute a percentage even 2% so as to bring commitment and ownership" (Fon 2024).

Recommendation from Field Actors

The aforementioned civil society leaders also had very poignant messages to address to the international community in times of humanitarian crises as Mangzha said:

> Civil society organizations (CSOs) play a vital role in protecting civilians during times of crisis. We are often the first responders, providing essential services when government and international aid are delayed or insufficient. Our deep connections with local communities enable us to deliver aid more effectively and to address the unique needs of different groups, such as women and children. The global community must recognize and support the work of CSOs, as we are essential partners in achieving sustainable peace and recovery in conflict zones.
>
> (Fon 2024)

Tiyang on his part emphasized that: "CSO needs to be financially empower to be able contribute solutions to the victims since they live in the very society where the victims are found" (Fon 2024b).

Conclusion

This chapter has highlighted the critical role that African civil society organizations (CSOs) play in responding to humanitarian crises in various sub-regions of the continent, focusing on the Lake Chad Basin, the Anglophone regions of

Cameroon, and the Central African Republic. The key findings demonstrate that CSOs have been instrumental in providing immediate relief, advocating for human rights, and promoting peacebuilding initiatives, often in extremely challenging and dangerous environments. Despite these efforts, CSOs face significant obstacles, including security risks, limited resources, and governmental restrictions.

The situation in Nigeria shows how corruption and uncoordinated efforts can undermine the effectiveness of humanitarian interventions. In Cameroon, CSOs have navigated shrinking civic spaces and intimidation, yet continue to push for peace and relief. In the Central African Republic, the innovative inter-religious cooperation among CSOs underscores the importance of local faith-based initiatives in fostering social cohesion amidst conflict. Reflecting on the importance of CSOs, it is clear that they fill critical gaps left by governmental and international actors, often being the first responders in crises and providing tailored, culturally sensitive interventions. Their proximity to affected communities and deep understanding of local contexts enable them to address the complex humanitarian needs more effectively than external actors might.

In conclusion, while African CSOs have made significant contributions to mitigating the effects of humanitarian crises, there is still much work to be done to support and amplify their efforts. Investing in the resilience and capacity of these organizations will be key to ensuring more effective and sustainable responses to future crises on the continent.

References

Abdullahi, I. 2020. "Intrastate Conflict and International Peacekeeping Operations in the Central African Republic (CAR)." *International Journal of Research and Innovation in Social Science* 4 (11): 265–77.

Abdullahi, M., and A. I. Chikaji. 2020. "Socio-Economic Development in Crises Ravaged Areas: A Study on the Adverse Effects of Humanitarian Support by Non-Governmental Organisations in Maiduguri, Nigeria." *Asia Proceedings of Social Sciences* 6 (1): 69–74.

Abdulmalik, J. O., A. M. C. Dahiru, M. S. Jidda, M. A. Wakil, and O. O. Omigbodun. 2019. "Boko Haram Insurgency and Nigeria's Mental Health Response." In *An International Perspective on Disasters and Children's Mental Health*, 45–61. Springer.

Adeakin, I., S. Gray, and O. Madu. 2021. "The Role of NGOs in the Boko Haram Conflict: Have NGO Activities in Northeast Nigeria Prolonged the Conflict?" In *Boko Haram's Terrorist Campaign in Nigeria*, 145–58. Routledge.

Ager, J., E. Fiddian-Qasmiyeh, and A. Ager. 2015. "Local Faith Communities and the Promotion of Resilience in Contexts of Humanitarian Crisis." *Journal of Refugee Studies* 28 (2): 202–21.

Amalu, N. S. 2015. "Impact of Boko Haram Insurgency on Human Security in Nigeria." *Global Journal of Social Sciences* 14 (1): 35–42.

Annan, N., M. Beseng, G. Crawford, and J. K. Kewir. 2021. "Civil Society, Peacebuilding from Below and Shrinking Civic Space: The Case of Cameroon's 'Anglophone' Conflict." *Conflict, Security & Development* 21 (6): 697–725.

Ashu, G. M. 2020. "The Impact of the Anglophone Conflict on Women and Children and Their Advocacy for Peace in Cameroon." *Gender and Behaviour* 18 (1): 14829–44.

Awosusi, A. E. 2017. "Aftermath of Boko Haram Violence in the Lake Chad Basin: A Neglected Global Health Threat." *BMJ Global Health* 2 (1): e000193.

Buanango, M. A., V. A. D. S. Ferreira, and M. R. M. de Oliveira. 2020. "Novo coronavírus SARS-CoV-2 e o agravamento da insegurança alimentar em países africanos com histórico de eventos climáticos e de conflitos armados." *Revista Simbiologias* 12 (16).

Campbell, H., and H. Nair. 2014. "Humanitarian Crises Due to Natural Disasters and Armed Conflict." *Journal of the Royal College of Physicians of Edinburgh* 44 (3): 216–17.

Chaplowe, S. G., and R. B. Engo-Tjega. 2007. "Civil Society Organizations and Evaluation: Lessons from Africa." *Evaluation* 13 (2): 257–74.

DeMattee, A. J. 2019. "Toward a Coherent Framework: A Typology and Conceptualization of CSO Regulatory Regimes." *Nonprofit Policy Forum* 9 (4): 20180011. (De Gruyter).

Dunne, P., and G. Mhone. 2003. *Africa's Crises: Recent Analysis of Armed Conflicts and Natural Disasters in Africa* (No. 5). International Labour Office.

Edoun, E. I., R. A. Balgah, and C. Mbohwa. 2015. "The Impact of Effective Management of Natural Disasters for Africa's Development." *Economic Research-Ekonomska istraživanja* 28 (1): 924–38.

Ehwarieme, W., and N. Umukoro. 2015. "Civil Society and Terrorism in Nigeria: A Study of the Boko Haram Crisis." *International Journal on World Peace* 32 (3).

Emmanuelar, I. 2015. "Insurgency and Humanitarian Crises in Northern Nigeria: The Case of Boko Haram." *African Journal of Political Science and International Relations* 9 (7): 284–96.

Engwari, M. C., and A. F. Njiei. 2021. "NGOs Interventions in the Care Provided to Internally Displaced Persons (IDPS): The Case of Community Initiative for Sustainable Development (COMINSUD) in the North West Region, Cameroon." *International Journal of Scientific Advances* 2 (4): 479–86.

Eribo, S. 2021. "COVID-19 and African Civil Society Organizations: Impact and Responses." *Alliance for African Partnership Perspectives* 1 (1): 147–55.

Essia, U., and A. Yearoo. 2009. "Strengthening Civil Society Organizations/Government Partnership in Nigeria." *International NGO Journal* 4 (9): 368–74.

Eze, C. B. 2016. "The Role of CSOS in Promoting Human Rights Protection, Mass Atrocities Prevention, and Civilian Protection in Armed Conflicts." *Global Responsibility to Protect* 8 (2–3): 249–69.

Fisseha, M. 2018. "The Roles of the Civil Society and International Humanitarian Organisations in Managing Refugees Crisis in the Middle East and North Africa (MENA) Region." *Journal of Mediterranean Knowledge* 3 (1): 61–80.

Fon, N. N. A. 2024. "Interview with Ms. Afiniki Mangzha Executive Director, Integrated Women and Youth Empowerment Centre (IWAYEC)." Personal. August 14.

Ford, E. 2013a. *Learning the Lessons? Assessing the Response to the 2012 Food Crisis in the Sahel to Build Resilience for the Future*. Vol. 168. Oxfam.

Ford, E. 2013b. *Food for Thought: A Civil Society Assessment on the State of Play of the Implementation of the Charter for Food Crisis Prevention and Management in the Sahel and West Africa*. Oxfam.

Gang, K. B. A., J. O'Keeffe, and L. Roberts. 2023. "Cross-Sectional Survey in Central African Republic Finds Mortality 4-Times Higher than UN Statistics: How Can We Not Know the Central African Republic is in Such an Acute Humanitarian Crisis?" *Conflict and Health* 17 (1): 21.

Glasius, M. 2009. " 'We Ourselves, We Are Part of the Functioning': The ICC, Victims, and Civil Society in the Central African Republic." *African Affairs* 108 (430): 49–67.

Idika-Kalu, C. 2020. "The Socioeconomic Impact of the Boko Haram Insurgency in the Lake Chad Basin Region." In *Terrorism and Developing Countries*. IntechOpen.

Illo, F., M. D. Akanmu, and N. Osman. 2023. "The Impact of Human Security and Terrorism on Nigeria Economy: A Case of Insurgency." *Jurnal Ekonomi Pembangunan: Kajian Masalah Ekonomi dan Pembangunan* 24 (1): 77–94.

International Crisis Group. 2022. "Rebels, Victims, Peacebuilders: Women in Cameroon's Anglophone Conflict." https://www.crisisgroup.org/africa/central-africa/cameroon/rebels-victims-peacebuilders-women-cameroons-anglophone-conflict

Iwu, H. N. 2022. "Chapter 18 Foreign Aid to Africa Since 1940." In *Africa in Global History: A Handbook*, edited by T. Falola and M. Salau, 335–54. Berlin and Boston, MA: De Gruyter Oldenbourg. https://doi.org/10.1515/9783110678017-019

KAICIID. 2024. "Plateforme des Confessions Religieuses de Centrafrique (PCRC)." https://www.kaiciid.org/what-we-do/we-convene/platform/plateforme-des-confessions-religieuses-de-centrafrique-pcrc

Kane, M. 2014. "Interreligious Violence in the Central African Republic: An Analysis of the Causes and Implications." *African Security Review* 23 (3): 312–17.

Kuehne, A., and L. Roberts. 2021. "Learning from Health Information Challenges in the Central African Republic: Where Documenting Health and Humanitarian Needs Requires Fresh Approaches." *Conflict and Health* 15 (1): 68.

Loretti, A., and Y. Tegegn. (1996) 1997. "Disasters in Africa: Old and New Hazards and Growing Vulnerability." *World Health Statistics Quarterly* 49 (3/4): 179–84.

Magiti, E. M. 2005. "The Civil Society and Humanitarian Assistance to Internally Displaced Persons in Africa." Doctoral diss.

Mahadevia, G. K. 2021. "Natural Disasters and Weak Government Institutions: Creating a Vicious Cycle That Ensnares Developing Countries." *Law and Development Review* 14 (1): 59–104.

Mahony, C. 2014. "An Inter-Religious Humanitarian Response in the Central African Republic." *Forced Migration Review* 48.

Mahony, C. 2024. "An Inter-Religious Humanitarian Response in the Central African Republic." https://www.fmreview.org/mahony/

Malhouni, Y., and C. Mabrouki. 2024. "Mitigating Risks and Overcoming Logistics Challenges in Humanitarian Deployment to Conflict Zones: Evidence from the DRC and CAR." *Journal of Humanitarian Logistics and Supply Chain Management* 14 (3): 225–46.

Mayhew, S. H., P. M. Kyamusugulwa, K. Kihangi Bindu, P. Richards, C. Kiyungu, and D. Balabanova. 2021. "Responding to the 2018–2020 Ebola Virus Outbreak in the Democratic Republic of the Congo: Rethinking Humanitarian Approaches." *Risk Management and Healthcare Policy*: 1731–47.

Moinina, V., and A. P. Ngoh. 2020. "The Role of the Civil Society in Conflicts: The Anglo-Phone Crisis in Cameroon." *Akdeniz havzası ve afrika medeniyetleri dergisi* 2 (2): 26–36.

Muntoh, E. M. 2020. "An Appraisal of the Involvement of Humanitarian Missions in Cameroon's Conflict Zones (North-West and South-West Regions)." *International Journal of Legal Studies (IJOLS)* 8 (2): 147–66.

Neumayr, M., M. Meyer, M. Pospíšil, U. Schneider, and I. Malý. 2009. The Role of Civil Society Organisations in Different Nonprofit Regimes: Evidence from Austria and the Czech Republic." In *Civil Society in Comparative Perspective*, 167–96. Emerald Group Publishing Limited.

Newey, A. 2024. "Religion, Peace, and Conflict in the Central African Republic: Can Faith-Based Peacebuilding De-Escalate Violence in Christian and Muslim Communities?" *Journal of Intersectional Justice* 2024: 1–11.

Nyadera, I. N., B. Wandwkha, and B. Agwanda. 2021. "Not the Time to Take Chances! Why African Governments' Response to COVID 19 Matters." *Global Social Welfare* 8: 137–40.

Okoli, A. C., and P. Iortyer. 2014. "Terrorism and Humanitarian Crisis in Nigeria: Insights from Boko Haram Insurgency." *Global Journal of Human Social Science* 14 (1): 39–49.

Ollong, K. A. 2021. "Irregular Ecologies: An Assessment of the Socio-Economic Implications of the Anglophone Crisis in Cameroon." *International Journal of Public and Private Perspectives on Healthcare, Culture, and the Environment (IJPPPHCE)* 5 (1): 29–45.

Prendergast, J. 1997. *Crisis Response: Humanitarian Band-Aids in Sudan and Somalia*. London: Pluto Press.

Rainey, S., K. Wakunuma, and B. Stahl. 2017. "Civil Society Organisations in Research: A Literature-Based Typology." *VOLUNTAS: International Journal of Voluntary and Nonprofit Organizations* 28: 1988–2010.

Sacks, A., and M. Levi. 2010. "Measuring Government Effectiveness and its Consequences for Social Welfare in Sub-Saharan African Countries." *Social Forces* 88 (5): 2325–51.

Samah, W. 2021. “Mediating Protection of Forcibly Displaced Populations in the Frontlines of the Central African Republic.” In *National Protection of Internally Displaced Persons in Africa: Beyond the Rhetoric*, 13–25. Springer.

Samah, W., and E. S. Tata. 2021. “Straddled between Government Forces and Armed Separatists: The Plight of Internally Displaced Persons from the Anglophone Regions of Cameroon.” In *National Protection of Internally Displaced Persons in Africa: Beyond the Rhetoric*, 73–92. Springer.

Sayem, G. W. 2020. “La question des déplacés forcés de la “Crise Anglophone” au Cameroun depuis 2016.” *Journal of the African Literature Association* 14 (2): 307–22.

Schneider, M., and V. Ferguson. 2020. *Central African Republic*. National Accounts Statistics: Main Aggregates and Detailed Tables 2019. United Nations, Department of Economic and Social Affairs.

Verkoren, W., and M. van Leeuwen. 2014. “Civil Society in Fragile Contexts.” In *The Handbook of Global Security Policy*, 463–81. Springer.

Wamai, R. G. 2013. “Civil Society’s Response to the HIV/AIDS Crisis in Africa.” In *The Handbook of Civil Society in Africa*, 361–98. New York: Springer.

4 Local Civil Society and Qatar's Diplomacy of Humanitarian Assistance to the Gaza Strip

Hani Albasoos

Introduction

This chapter examines the role of Qatari diplomacy through its humanitarian assistance to the Gaza Strip during the humanitarian crisis striking the local society and dividing the Gaza Strip owing to the military campaigns and wars of the last two decades. The term humanitarian diplomacy was used at the beginning of the twentieth century, and the actual practice of the concept began to spread after World War II within a new context where diplomatic operations were developed on the basis of the civil element of new wars, intrastate conflicts, and the participation of armed forces and non-state armed groups in conflicts. Both of state and non-state actors involve in negotiations as a part of humanitarian diplomacy activities. The latter is originated from humanitarian aid, the alleviation of human suffering and achieving security, and cessation of violations of human rights in countries which are affected by conflicts. The new approach to humanity leads to the possibility of reaching people in need and providing them with relief and emergency aid through mediation, negotiations, and humanitarian diplomacy (Bogatyreva 2023).

Humanitarian diplomacy is the use of high-level engagement efforts to influence parties in armed conflict and their allies to achieve humanitarian goals. It requires relationship development at the highest level to coordinate emergency relief and humanitarian responses. It is the process of influencing decision-makers and opinion leaders to act in the interests of vulnerable people at all times while adhering to core humanitarian values. Humanitarian diplomacy requires new methods to engage constructively and positively to influence actors in armed conflicts who have the capacity to take actions. This is where humanitarian diplomacy offers a valuable tool, enhancing capacity and influencing leaders to address humanitarian challenges (Pease 2020).

Humanitarian diplomacy aims to achieve humanitarian goals through diplomatic means and strives to mobilize public and governmental support and resources for humanitarian operations and programs. In addition, it also aims building effective partnerships with players in the conflict zones to respond to the needs of vulnerable people to address both short- and long-term needs.

DOI: 10.4324/9781003565048-4

Humanitarian diplomacy can be used for a variety of humanitarian purposes such as emergency relief operations and medical aid to local communities, in coordination with leaders and individuals at different levels and responsibilities. Thus, humanitarian diplomacy can be used to influence state, non-state actors, and armed groups to positively respond to global humanitarian issues (Jonsson 2002).

For humanitarian diplomacy to succeed, it is necessary to understand the geopolitical landscape and actors in the conflict in order to identify opportunities for agreements. This depends on an established and solid network of relevant contacts that can be mobilized to support negotiations to achieve sustainable humanitarian support. This requires the ability to have leveraged relationships with the civil society, public institutions, and armed groups to ensure that these relationships are utilized in pursuit of the same shared humanitarian goals. Humanitarian diplomacy also depends on the willingness of the parties in the conflict to negotiate in good faith and their ability to ensure that their efforts are unified in this direction. This means that humanitarian diplomacy does not always succeed but can still help lay the foundations for future successes such as achieving a ceasefire, truce, or other shared humanitarian goals (Bogatyreva 2023).

Krasheninnikova (2019) provided an analytical framework for the practice of humanitarian diplomacy. He related the formation of diplomacy to internal conflicts that are characterized by the escalation of hostilities and exposing traditional diplomacy of being incapable of resolving humanitarian problems. Complex emergencies have occurred in a variety of settings and have been accompanied by forced displacement or mass displacement of people, the collapse of economies and state infrastructure, the spread of internal conflicts, epidemics, famine, and lack of access to quality health care. In such situations, humanitarian diplomacy can play as a main instrument to force governments to encourage international organizations to respond to crises in a timely manner, with due respect for international law.

Development of the Concept

The first humanitarian rules, in ancient times, were associated with granting immunity to those who had to recover the bodies of dead soldiers and were linked to the first forms of asylum, the exchange of prisoners, and basic forms of human treatments. Humanitarian positions have evolved over centuries against the backdrop of changing ideological ideas about the value of human life. The International Committee of the Red Cross, established in 1863, began to play a leading role in developing ideas about the protection and dignity of affected populations. These principles became a common ideological basis for international humanitarian organizations. In the twentieth century, the suffering and misery caused by new destructive technologies of warfare led to the signing of the Geneva Conventions of 1949 and their Additional Protocols. The development of international humanitarian law became one of the achievements of diplomacy and contributed to the formation of humanitarianism of NGOs. Humanitarian diplomacy is an independent field of diplomatic activity that was formed after the end of the Cold War and focused on maximizing support for humanitarian operations and building the necessary partnerships with relevant organizations to achieve humanitarian goals despite the different objectives of the players and participants in situations of armed conflict.

However, humanitarian diplomacy is not limited to the activities of the Red Cross and Red Crescent Societies and the International Committee of the Red Cross. It is carried out by a wide range of nongovernmental organizations that aim to relieve people from suffering and address the urgent needs of victims of armed conflicts. As an analytical tool, Smith (2007) presented ideas about humanitarian diplomacy in terms of its goals, functions, methods, and subjects.

First, the concept contains an internal contradiction: humanitarian action and diplomacy are separate and sometimes conflicting activities. If the goal of the diplomat is to ensure the national interests and security of the country, then humanitarians prioritize human life and the formation of a humanitarian space. Second, humanitarian diplomacy in modern conflicts has become a fact, as humanitarians have to negotiate with state and non-state actors, using the art of persuasion and compromise to achieve their legitimate goals. Third, humanitarian diplomacy is indispensable, as actors involved in a conflict zone cannot remain neutral, and usually political imperatives supersede humanitarian necessities. Smith (2007) believes that these types are not mutually exclusive, and each contributes to the interpretation of the whole concept. Hence, humanitarian diplomacy is defined as "the pursuit of international interests by peaceful means". Humanitarian diplomacy is a broad and complex element of the foreign policy of modern states, and international organizations aim to reduce challenges and ensure the security and protection of people and focus on emergencies, not on changing laws and practices within the framework of human rights and diplomacy (Pease 2020).

Roles and Responsibilities

Humanitarian diplomacy has been formed as an independent track of diplomatic activities, focusing on issues of protection and assistance to populations in conditions of natural and man-made disasters. Examples of humanitarian crises caused by natural disasters and the growth of internal armed conflicts, which have become protracted and exacerbated, confirm the contribution of humanitarian diplomacy as a form of transnational public activity that promotes the interaction of various actors in order to achieve constructive results in protecting and assisting the affected population. Despite the ethical, legal, and operational challenges that humanitarian diplomacy faces, it is an effective tool for creating humanitarian space, negotiations, and expanding the scope of humanitarian action. Guided by humanitarian principles, many stakeholders can engage and interact with actors such as non-state armed groups, negotiations with which are neglected in the implementation of many other forms of diplomacy (Constantinou, Kerr, and Sharp 2016).

Humanitarian diplomacy is characterized by its ability to deal with emergency situations and overcome deep differences to resolve situations that were previously considered intractable. The UN Secretary-General stressed the need to constructively reorient tools and methods, including diplomacy, in order to work on preventing crises. This requires a significant increase in the efforts of states and organizations to prevent conflicts and manage crises and the use of global and regional forums for the exchange of information and continuously monitoring such events. Since most conflicts are of an internal nature, it is important for neutral humanitarian actors to engage in dialogue with states and non-state armed groups, in order to enhance their acceptance, understanding, and implementation of obligations under international humanitarian law and international human rights law. Humanitarian diplomacy aims to reduce human suffering and bridge the gap between humanitarian assistance and development. It includes providing assistance and trying to eradicate poverty, reduce forced displacement of populations, support refugees and migrants, fill gaps in education, as well as struggle to end physical violence. This requires bridging the gap between humanitarian assistance and development (Himpel and Ayad 2024).

Recent analyses of the concept of humanitarian diplomacy show that there is a universal understanding of the context of modern approaches of diplomacy and security. The framework of these concepts revolves around the basic principles of humanity, neutrality, and independence.

Tools and Actors

Humanitarian diplomacy aims to persuade actors in conflict zones to compromise, where diplomats perform three main functions: representation, communication, and negotiation. Humanitarian diplomacy uses traditional diplomatic tools in gathering information in favor of achieving humanitarian goals and protecting human rights. They enter into dialogue to persuade decision-makers and interact with the media to ensure public awareness of the situations in which they are involved. In fact, the ability to negotiate is the most important skill in humanitarian work and humanitarian diplomacy is based on the rules of international humanitarian law, international refugee law, and international human rights law. Humanitarian actors play an important role in identifying problems, forming ideas about the conflict and its consequences, and proposing political ways to overcome them (Bogatyreva 2023).

There is a current political trend toward recognizing negotiations with non-state armed groups as a legitimate practice and an integral part of humanitarian work. In this regard, a state actor may play an important role in bringing the conflicting parties to the negotiating table and reaching agreements. Accordingly, the social power of diplomacy has been recognized which can transform the behavior of conflict participants into being a more civilized and humane one. Engaging with non-state groups can transform a conflict into a nonviolent form, as it is believed that the participation of the enemy in negotiations can end the use of force. International law obliges governments to provide people living in the territories under their control with access to humanitarian assistance and protection, as humanitarian action aims to prevent, reduce, and stop violations (Constantinou, Kerr, and Sharp (2016).

Humanitarian diplomacy is closely linked to the activities of the United Nations in peacekeeping. The focus of the UN Security Council is on emergencies and providing continuous access to humanitarian assistance and protection. These objectives are implemented in diplomatic practice on the ground, where negotiations are held to reach ceasefires, build humanitarian corridors, and respect humanitarian law. Humanitarian diplomacy is based on the coordinated interaction between state and non-state actors. Humanitarian practice is not only about providing assistance and support to people affected by emergencies, armed conflicts, climate change, or poverty but also about rebuilding societies without compromising development prospects and achieving the sustainable development goals. Humanitarian diplomacy of states, seeking to achieve the goal of creating a positive national image, uses a range of different tools and may include humanitarian aid, social policy, and economic and technological assistance in the context of sustainable development (Jonsson 2002).

Armed conflicts and global humanitarian problems have required the expansion of the scope of governmental and nongovernmental humanitarian actors in a professional manner at the international level to utilize traditional diplomatic means—dialogue, negotiations, and mediation for settlements, in addition to advocating for the representation and protection of the rights of victims of conflicts and crises. States' humanitarian diplomacy is an important element as soft power, providing aid to affected regions and protecting vulnerable people, depends on the course of the state's foreign policy and on the international commitments taken to reduce suffering and human rights violations. Diplomacy has acquired an unprecedented complexity, especially with the emergence of new diplomats—private companies, humanitarian organizations, and transnational political actors—who work from above, from below, and in parallel with the state (Constantinou, Kerr, and Sharp 2016).

First: The International Committee of the Red Cross: the ICRC continues to play a major role in the humanitarian field. Its autonomy is defined by the mandate granted to it by states joining the Geneva Conventions of 1949 to become a functional international legal personality that allows it to obtain diplomatic status and observer status in the UN General Assembly. However, this international legal personality is limited to the tasks of providing relief and protection of victims in conflicts. It includes a number of activities in the fields of health, sanitation, food, security, searching for missing persons, etc. (UN Document 2026).

Second: The United Nations: humanitarian assistance has been provided by the United Nations High Commissioner for Refugees, the Office of the United Nations High Commissioner for Human Rights, UNICEF, the United Nations Development Program, the World Food Program, and the World Health Organization, whose staff can rightly be called "humanitarian diplomats" and enjoy diplomatic immunity. In 1991, humanitarian activities within the UN became more institutionalized with the creation of the Office for the Coordination of Humanitarian Affairs (OCHA). It provides the clearest example of the integration of humanitarian goals and practices into UN institutions. In 2005, OCHA launched a humanitarian reform initiative and proposed strengthening the role of the Office as the body responsible for the overall organization of the global humanitarian system in order to achieve maximum cooperation and interaction between various actors. In addition, it was planned to create a collective UN response mechanism, consisting of specialized groups with the participation of UN agencies, the International Committee of the Red Cross, international organizations, and NGOs in areas such as food security, early recovery, emergency shelter, nutrition, water, sanitation and hygiene, health, and education (Bogatyreva 2023).

Third: States: the use of the term humanitarian diplomacy is not limited to civil society organizations and UN agencies. It is being increasingly used by states in conjunction with the growth of humanitarian assistance on a global scale. Humanitarian diplomacy of states is of great interest to researchers, as it identifies national and regional models of humanitarian diplomacy, strengthening the positions of states and achieving regional leadership in humanitarian actions. Humanitarian diplomacy, as an element of foreign policy, provides states with an opportunity to express international sympathy and solidarity and can enhance a state's reputation and provide valuable tools for building trust and cooperation. However, the inclusion of humanitarian diplomacy in foreign policy can lead to conflicts due to contradictions between humanitarian goals and broader national interests (Smith 2007).

Qatar Humanitarian Diplomacy

The concept of humanitarian diplomacy often includes aid and mediation as two sides of the same coin. Humanitarian diplomacy can require the exercise of financial leverage while simultaneously building soft power. Of all Gulf states' donors, Qatar has been the most active in ensuring its participation in high-level diplomatic and mediation efforts (Aljazeera.net 2023). Qatar's diplomatic record, both in direct mediation and in providing a venue for negotiations, is impressive, not only because of the country's apparent small geographic size but also because of the lasting compromises that Qatari diplomats have achieved. Long before hosting the Taliban–US talks in Doha, Qatar played a key role in finalizing the 2008 Doha Agreement during the Lebanon conflict, the 2008 ceasefire in the Yemen conflict, the 2010 ceasefire in Sudan, and the 2012 Doha Agreement in the Fatah–Hamas political struggle. Qatar brokered the US–Iran prisoner swap in August 2023. The deal included the release of five Iranians and led to the lifting of the embargo on $6 billion in Iranian assets. It also resulted in the transfer of Iranian funds frozen in South Korea to Qatari banks. In return, Iran released five American prisoners who arrived in Doha and were then transferred to the United States. Further diplomatic successes were seen in Western Sahara, Algeria, Eritrea, Ethiopia, Djibouti, and Somalia, among others (Gargoli 2024).

Trusted Partner and Honest Mediator

Qatar has earned its current title as a "trusted partner" through mediation. There are many examples of Qatari mediation roles, as it has happened where Qatar has mediated between states and other actors, in partnership with other allies and international organizations, based on a commitment to diplomatic efforts in accordance with the principles of the United Nations and international law. The tools and capabilities that have made Qatar known as a successful mediator are a complex set of different things such as strong political connections on a wide scale, huge financial resources, reliability, and neutrality. Engaging in mediation has not been an easy task for Qatar, as unexpected challenges arise from several geopolitical factors. The principle of neutrality also sometimes requires enormous efforts and resources to resolve issues and bring parties back to negotiations, including shuttle diplomacy, huge financial resources, and multilateral diplomacy (Barakat 2012).

Qatar is emerging as a hub for preventive diplomacy, as Qatar has now become an international diplomatic center for peace negotiations, mediation, and conflict resolution. Qatar's position has been affirmed during many international crises. The State of Qatar has gained a global reputation for its initiatives in resolving conflicts and providing humanitarian aid and educational initiatives to those in need around the world. Qatar has directed a large part of its international humanitarian aid toward addressing hunger and food shortages in different regions. The Qatar Fund for Development has signed agreements with the World Food Program, the Food and Agriculture Organization, and the World Health Organization to provide a large financial contribution to secure food and medical aid for millions of people in different countries. Qatar Charity has launched various projects to deliver aid to the displaced people, meet their basic needs, and provide them with shelter assistance in different regions (The Peninsula 2022).

The United States and Qatar have deep and multifaceted cooperation in many fields, including counterterrorism, investment, trade, economics, diplomacy, culture, education, and health. With its unique diplomatic capabilities, Qatar has helped Washington address many foreign policy challenges in the Middle East. Qatar's foreign policy initiatives in the field of humanitarian projects and comprehensive conflict resolution cannot be viewed as separate from the interests of its security guarantor, the United States. Afghanistan is perhaps the most prominent example in this regard. After the withdrawal of the US-led coalition, Qatar played a unique and indispensable role in facilitating contacts with the new Taliban government and ensuring a peaceful evacuation process. In late 2021, US Secretary of State Antony Blinken announced that Qatar would represent Washington's interests in Afghanistan for the foreseeable future. Building on its traditionally strong ties with Washington, this development elevated US–Qatar relations, reaffirming a set of shared security and economic interests (Himpel and Ayad 2024).

Humanitarian and Diplomatic Hub

Along with a range of long-term progressive measures toward economic diversification, infrastructure, and human and community development in almost every sector, Qatar's calculations have included establishing itself as a humanitarian and diplomatic hub. Government entities, private organizations, and individuals are engaged in charitable work and humanitarian assistance. The country carries out global humanitarian assistance activities at the international level and with multilateral organizations. A prime example is Qatar Airways, the country's national carrier, which is a strategic partner of the UNHCR. Qatar Airways Cargo takes this pledge very seriously, as humanitarian relief shipments, once booked, are never replaced by commercial shipments, even those contracted prior to departure. A humanitarian mission has gone significantly beyond the airline's philosophy and the way it delivers its work (Qatar Tribune 2024). Relying on Doha's infrastructure at Hamad International Airport, Qatar Airways Cargo has also been instrumental in providing many countries around the world with much-needed COVID-19 supplies during the most severe periods of the pandemic. In addition to its air transport capabilities, Qatar also uses maritime transport to make in-kind aid contributions globally. In the summer of 2021, for example, when India became aware of the emergence of the Delta variant, the country delivered 1,200 metric tons of liquid medical oxygen to support its healthcare system (Al-Kawari 2023).

Qatar is using a multifaceted aid model. On the one hand, it openly provides bilateral aid to some countries of its own free will and enthusiasm. On the other hand, it cooperates extensively with multilateral organizations such as the United Nations, which clearly reflects the country's enhanced commitment to multilateralism. Among other engagements, Qatar supports the United Nations Office for the Coordination of Humanitarian Affairs (UNOCHA), which brings together humanitarian actors to improve and coordinate coherent responses to emergencies around the world (Qatar International Media Office 2024). Like other Gulf donor countries, Qatar prefers to provide bilateral humanitarian aid. Two main public agencies are deployed to implement this: Qatar Charity and the Qatar Red Crescent Society. Qatar Charity has often been the first responder in times of crisis. The organization has been recognized as an important partner of the United Nations High Commissioner for Refugees; it has contributed more than $48 million to displaced persons and refugees since 2012, reaching more than one million beneficiaries during that period. Qatar Red Crescent Society (QRCS) is a member of the International Red Cross and Red Crescent Movement and was founded in 1978, making it the first voluntary charitable organization in Qatar. In addition to its role as a charitable group, QRCS also negotiates access to populations in difficult conflict zones, such as in Sudan, Somalia, Afghanistan, or Palestine (Aljazeera.net. 2024).

Palestinian Civil Society of Gaza

Civil society plays an important political role in humanitarian negotiations aimed at resolving modern conflicts, similar to the role of the United Nations in establishing a humanitarian partnership with nongovernmental organizations. Modern humanitarian practice requires a multi-dimension and complex approach that includes humanitarian, political, social, and economic aid in the context of a sustainable development model. The use of diplomatic tools, primarily, negotiations, has a positive impact on the effectiveness of humanitarian activities in armed conflicts and crisis situations such as in the Gaza Strip. Yet, there are significant difficulties in coordination and cooperation between different parties to deliver humanitarian aid in conflict zones, as cooperation between public institutions and civil society organizations (CSOs) is a key element and an essential approach in conflict zones when addressing the humanitarian crisis. Therefore, this research provides an updated analysis of Qatari diplomatic engagement with local civil society, mainly in the Gaza Strip, focusing on the challenges, opportunities, and lessons learned, especially amid the unstable conditions and the enormous challenges and uncertainties in managing the humanitarian situation during the armed conflict.

There have been three types of institutions that provide assistance to poor families in the Gaza Strip: official institutions affiliated with the Palestinian National Authority, Palestinian civil society organizations (CSOs), and international or foreign organizations. Prior to the October war on Gaza, 11.5% of CSOs were international, compared to 88.5% that were local. Yet, Gaza's CSOs did not have a decisive role in managing the aid, as the Ministry of Social Development (both Gaza and Ramallah) was the main controller of the aid management process, in addition to international institutions such as the United Nations Relief and Works Agency (UNRWA). The work of Gaza CSOs in humanitarian aid came through their donor partners, and within the available quotas allocated by the Ministry of Social Development or international partners (Costantini, Salima, and Isa 2015).

CSOs, mainly humanitarian organizations, have been strengthening the steadfastness of citizens of Gaza in the face of the fierce Israeli military policies and contentious siege for the past two decades. They have a great role to play to quickly recover from the tragic humanitarian situation, overcome the shocks, and be flexible in transforming their activities and programs to provide relief to the people of Gaza (Abu Matar 2012).

Nonetheless, Gaza CSOs were not unified in distributing aid, as the criteria were not uniform, principally after the October war. Some organizations adopted the displacement criterion in distributing aid, and others relied on their beneficiary lists—that is, before the war to benefit from their aid. Other organizations went to criteria related to their specialization in advance in women's organizations and organizations for people with disabilities to distribute their aid. In fact, the lack of the necessary structure and standards of CSOs and the local community representatives, especially those related to the distribution of aid, resulted in many problems related to their transparency. There has been lack of efficiency and transparency in the response to the need of civil society in Gaza in accordance with the requirements of justice in the humanitarian aid, including commitment to distribution standards. In addition, a state of confusion, the absence of clear policies in times of emergency and crisis, and the inability to keep up with the humanitarian disaster resulting from the Israeli war also have caused chaos in Gaza and disruption of the work of CSOs. The humanitarian environment in the Strip, with its various formations, primarily Palestinian civil society organizations, has witnessed a clear inability to cope with this catastrophe, which has led to the loss of most institutions. In addition, the aid distribution operations witnessed great difficulties in communication and interaction, which in turn reduced the opportunities for controlling the distribution operations.

It confirmed that Gaza CSOs should ensure that aid for distribution is based on the real needs for the target population and takes the special needs of some groups such as women, children, and people with disabilities in a way that helps preserve their health, dignity, and safety. Beneficiaries must receive clear information about the distribution and distribution sites must be accessible to all stakeholders and must meet security requirements. Distribution operations must also be fast and effective. The distribution of aid must be free of charge, and the population must be clearly informed of this prior to distribution (Amman 2024).

Humanitarian and Diplomatic Efforts during the Gaza War

Humanitarian aid is the backbone of Qatar's efforts to secure a leading role as an international mediator. While Qatar has repeatedly stressed the importance of separating politics from critical support for the Palestinian people, humanitarian aid has a long tradition in the Arab world. Humanitarian and development aid are intertwined and are not meant to be reciprocal, a notion that echoes Islamic concepts such as "zakat", a mandatory charitable contribution, and "sadaqah", which can be defined as a voluntary offering without asking for anything in return. Humanitarian aid from Qatar has become more transparent, and aid flows can be further accurately noticeable. At the same time, Qatar's aid to Gaza, while controversial in some corners, is likely to be among the largest and longest-standing pillars of the country's humanitarian and diplomatic efforts. Reuters reported that Doha's financial contributions to Gaza may have amounted to more than $1 billion since 2014, with another $500 million pledged in May 2021. In distributing aid, Qatar has worked with other stakeholders in the Israeli–Palestinian conflict—most notably the United States, the United Nations, and Israel—to ensure that its funding more effectively assists the civilian population in the Gaza Strip (Cafiero 2024).

Qatar has established itself as a major mediator in the Israeli–Palestinian conflict, leaving a clear sign on the map of mediation and peace talks, and resolving disputes. Doha's mediation efforts have earned it widespread international trust and credibility. Yet, there are mixed views in the United States about Qatar, where Doha has received some criticism from certain political elites and think tanks in Washington regarding the fact that Qatar has hosted the political leadership of Hamas since 2012. However, the official US–Qatar relations are unlikely to change as based on four dimensions: cultural, with American universities in Qatar; economic, with the massive amounts of investment made by American companies in the country; political, with close cooperation in a number of political and diplomatic fields; and security, with the presence of the US military base in Qatar. Besides, Washington has worked with Doha, for the past years, on many important cases, including Afghanistan, Iraq, Libya, Syria, Yemen, and Palestine (Cafiero 2024).

Qatari humanitarian diplomacy has been vital in light of this catastrophic humanitarian crisis that has been hitting the local community in the Strip due to the Israeli war. Qatar, as a main mediator in this war, is still trying to find a solution to the humanitarian challenges facing the Palestinian society. The Qatari role has been crucial in this conflict through its humanitarian and diplomatic efforts. Qatar works sincerely to provide humanitarian and relief aid in order to enhance its role in mediation, its efforts are clear and tangible in alleviating suffering and achieving permanent solutions, and it cooperates with regional countries to build joint and multilateral efforts to guide the region toward stability and peace (Demer 2023).

Qatar has a long diplomatic experience in the Israeli–Palestinian conflict, as it served as a diplomatic bridge between Israel and the Gaza-based military factions, mainly Hamas, in previous armed confrontations in 2014 and 2021. Over the years, Qatar has also used its resources and diplomatic influence to help Gaza deal with humanitarian challenges and energy issues. Given Qatar's past relationships with the parties involved, its long-standing role in Gaza, and its established record of achieving tangible results in previous wars between Israel and Gaza, Doha's role in mediating between Hamas and Israel is enormous (Cafiero 2024). Qatar has invested a great deal of diplomacy in an attempt to reach a ceasefire and prisoners' exchange between Hamas and Israel, addressing the humanitarian disaster in Gaza, and convince both sides to reach an end to the war. Qatari diplomatic work has achieved positive and tangible results. Qatar has engineered negotiations to stop the Israeli attacks, reduce escalation, stop the bloodshed, and protect civilians. Qatari efforts succeeded in reaching a ceasefire on 22nd November, paving the way for the exchange of dozens of prisoners and allowing the delivery of humanitarian convoys and relief aid, including fuel for humanitarian needs, to Gaza. In fact, without Qatari efforts, none of the detainees would have been released. Although the ceasefire did not last long, and the Israeli military attacks resumed. Yet, Qatar has continued its efforts to alleviate the suffering of more than two million Palestinians trapped in Gaza. US Secretary of State Antony Blinken visited Doha and praised Qatar's efforts (Qatar Tribune 2024).

Qatar has faced increasing criticism from Israeli officials over its crucial mediation role aimed at reaching a ceasefire and prisoners' exchange deal. This is despite Qatar's active role in securing the release of 109 Israeli prisoners in November 2023, under an agreement brokered by Doha and Cairo (Mason and Spetalnick 2024). In January 2024, Israeli Prime Minister Benjamin Netanyahu described Qatar's mediation position as "problematic" (Aljazeera.net. 2024). Later, in April, Israeli Economy Minister Nir Barkat accused Qatar of being "untrustworthy" and "posing a threat to peace" in an interview with Bloomberg (Gargoli 2024). These attempts aim to transform Qatar's role from an honest mediator to a pressure tool. Yet, the State of Qatar has maintained its role as an honest regional and international mediator throughout previous and current diplomatic efforts.

Thus, on April 17, Qatari Prime Minister and Foreign Minister Mohammed bin Abdulrahman Al Thani condemned such statements as being an exploitation of his country's diplomatic efforts. He stated, "Doha is in the process of evaluating its role in this mediation process", believing that this mediation is being misused for narrow political interests (Aljazeera.net. 2024). He reiterated Qatar's commitment to the role of an "honest mediator" between Israel and Hamas, emphasizing that it will not accept being used as a pressure tool by any party. Al Thani confirmed the Qatari role as a neutral mediator committed to integrity and rejects external interference of its mediation efforts. Thus, Qatar continued its mediation, where talks gained political momentum in May and again in August 2024 with support from the United States. However, the Israeli military attacks are ongoing on a wide-scale level in the whole Gaza Strip, forcing the US President to criticize the Israeli prime minister of not making enough efforts to reach a ceasefire deal (Mason and Spetalnick 2024).

In brief, the main task of these organizations is to negotiate with international or national players, act as a neutral intermediary, and help ensure that the voices of victims of armed conflicts are heard. Therefore, humanitarian diplomacy, in the restricted concept, is the activity of specialized organizations with political and military powers to negotiate and consciously perform their functions, based on the principles of independence, neutrality, and justice. Attempts to perceive humanitarian diplomacy as an activity limited only to specialized NGOs aimed at saving lives and alleviating suffering have not found much support in the literature.

Conclusion

The reality for millions of people suffering from conflicts, natural disasters, or situations of poverty and deprivation is that they have to fight for their life, dignity, security, equality, food, shelter, education, and health. The protracted and intractable nature of modern wars and the transfer of battlefields to urban environments have led to the killing of a large number of civilians, the spread of diseases, and the destruction of vital infrastructure, negatively impacting international efforts to achieve the sustainable development goals. Conflicts have increased significantly, requiring diplomatic efforts and parallel participation in negotiations by many actors: state and non-state actors and individual leaders with political or economic influence to link humanitarian diplomacy with development, peacebuilding, and conflict resolution while respecting most human rights. By combining humanitarian and relief assistance with mediation and negotiation, the State of Qatar has been able to forge a number of key partnerships with state and non-state actors to achieve its humanitarian and development goals in a sensible and effective manner. Given the complexity of modern geopolitics, financial aid often falls short of addressing the most critical problems in the developing world.

The State of Qatar has maintained credibility, reliability, and an authentic role in mediation at the regional and international levels. It has strengthened its role as a reliable mediator through relief work and humanitarian diplomacy. Qatar's humanitarian and diplomatic efforts have been remarkably consistent for decades. The country is gaining a more prominent position on the international stage, and it will properly make itself available as a center for dialogue and negotiation at the crossroads of East and West. The current situation in the Gaza Strip is described as a humanitarian disaster, where infrastructure, services, and educational institutions have been destroyed; and most homes have been demolished. Thus, Gaza will continue to require significant support from the international community. Qatar pledged that it will continue to play a vital role in this process, both in the immediate and long terms. Qatar has gained sufficient experience in the Palestinian issue, mainly on Palestinian national reconciliation, ceasefires with Israel, and humanitarian and relief aid. Qatar has gained high trust from all parties based on its credibility and professional role during the past years and is thus continuing mediation efforts and humanitarian and relief work for the Palestinian people.

The Israeli war on the Gaza Strip has imposed many challenges to local and international CSOs in managing the humanitarian aid in Gaza since October 2023. The war has destroyed all the necessities of life in the Gaza Strip, exceeding the capabilities of all official, civil, local, and international institutions to confront it and respond to the requirements of this wide-scale aggression that led to spreading chaos, fragmentation, and the systematic dismantling of the structures of Palestinian civil society organizations in the Strip. CSOs found themselves facing major challenges in responding to the humanitarian needs of more than two million Palestinian citizens. Many CSOs have refrained from playing any role in the current crisis and have closed their administrative and executive offices in the Strip. This may be due to the cessation of funding, because of the war, or as a result of incapability of responding to those needs, and there are some institutions whose level of response to humanitarian needs was not at the level of the crisis.

Despite various international humanitarian initiatives and the call of the UN Secretary-General to end the recent war on Gaza since October 2023, save people's lives, address humanitarian crises, and facilitate the delivery of vital supplies to those in need, the war still poses a real threat to humanity, where people suffer from poor services and infrastructure and a lack of health care facilities. Yet, the State of Qatar represents a living model of humanitarian diplomacy in Gaza by promoting humanitarian values and human rights, focusing on human rights, improving living conditions, enhancing protection for individuals and groups, and providing humanitarian aid and relief. The Qatari diplomacy has partially contributed to relieving some of the suffering in Gaza and bringing some hope to the population.

According to the expanded approach to the concept of humanitarian diplomacy, famous personalities, states, and international institutions participate in humanitarian diplomacy when its goal is to preserve human dignity. Humanitarian diplomacy cannot be reduced to humanitarian aid only; it involves intervention not only in armed conflicts but also in situations where people are at risk due to natural disasters, epidemics, or social crises. Organizations and states that provide access to affected populations, in addition to assistance and protection, resort to mediation and negotiations to interact with parties that are not always equal and often in conflict and post-conflict situations. They have to deal not only with official state bodies but also with the representatives of armed groups.

References

Abu Matar, M. 2012. *Contributions of Palestinian Civil Society Institutions to Ending the State of Division and Achieving National Reconciliation (2007–2010)*. Arab Center for Research and Policy Studies. https://www.dohainstitute.org (in Arabic)

Aljazeera.net. 2023. "Creative Humanitarian Diplomacy: Global Praise for Qatari Mediation at the Conclusion of the Doha Forum." Accessed 12 December 2023. https://www.aljazeera.net/politics (in Arabic)

Aljazeera.net. 2024. "Qatar Committed to Israel-Hamas Honest Mediator Role: Diplomatic Sources." Accessed 4 May 2024. https://www.aljazeera.com/news

Al-Kawari, A. 2023. "Humanitarian Diplomacy." *Asharq Newspaper*, November 28. https://al-sharq.com/ (in Arabic)

Amman (The Coalition for Integrity and Accountability-AMAN). 2024. "The Extent of Civil Society Institutions' Response to the Requirements of Justice in the Humanitarian Aid in Light of the War on the Gaza Strip, April 2024." https://www.aman-palestine.org/category-542/26125.html (in Arabic)

Barakat, S. 2012. *The Qatari Spring: Qatar's Emerging Role in Peacemaking, Kuwait Program on Development, Governance and Globalization in the Gulf States*. London: London School of Economics and Political Science. http://eprints.lse.ac.uk/59266/

Bogatyreva, O. 2023. "Humanitarian Diplomacy: Modern Concepts and Approaches." *Springer Nature* 92 (14), March 23.

Cafiero, G. 2024. "Why Qatar Is the Go-to Mediator in the Gaza War, and Beyond." *The News Arab*, April 29. https://www.newarab.com/analysis/why-qatar-go-mediator-gaza-war-and-beyond

Constantinou, C. M., P. Kerr, and P. Sharp. 2016. "Understanding Diplomatic Practice." In *The SAGE Handbook of Diplomacy*, edited by C. M. Constantinou, P. Kerr, and P. Sharp. London: SAGE.

Costantini, G., A. Salima, and M. Isa. 2015. "Analytical Survey Study of Civil Society Organisations in Palestine." January 28. https://www.eeas.europa.eu/sites/default/files/final_report_mapping_update_2015-ar.pdf (in Arabic)

Demer, A. 2023. "Qatar's Foreign Policy: Between Mediation and Humanitarian Development." *Türkiye News Agency*, December 18. https://tr.agency/news-177778 (in Arabic)

Gargoli, A. 2024. "Qatar Maintains Role as Honest Mediator in Gaza Talks, Rejects Attempts to Become 'Pressure Tool'." *Doha News*, May 6. https://dohanews.co/qatar-maintains-honest-mediator-role-in-gaza-talks-rejects-attempts-to-turn-into-pressure-tool (in Arabic)

Himpel, F., and K. Ayad. 2024. "Qatar's Growing Role as a Humanitarian and Diplomatic Hub." *Gulf International Forum*. Accessed May 18, 2024. https://gulfif.org/qatars-growing-role-as-a-humanitarian-and-diplomatic-hub/

Jonsson, C. 2002. "Diplomacy, Bargaining, and Negotiation." In *Handbook of International Relations*. London: SAGE.

Krasheninnikova, E. A. 2019. "Religious Diplomacy in the Settlement of the Afghan Conflict: Opportunities and Limitations, Vestnik RUDN." *International Relations* 19: 533–44.

Mason, J., and M. Spetalnick. 2024. "Biden Says Netanyahu Not Doing Enough to Secure Hostage Deal." *Reuters*, September 3. https://www.reuters.com/world/middle-east

Pease, K. K. 2020. "Introduction to Human Rights and Humanitarian Diplomacy." In *Human Rights and Humanitarian Diplomacy*. Manchester: Manchester University Press.

The Peninsula. 2022. "Qatar's Humanitarian Diplomacy." October 31. https://thepeninsulaqatar.com/editorial/31/10/2022/qatars-humanitarian-diplomacy

Qatar International Media Office. 2024. "Foreign Policy." Accessed September 11, 2024. https://imo.gov.qa/ar/priorities/foreign-policy/ (in Arabic)

Qatar Tribune. 2024. "Qatar Emerges as a Global Destination for Mediation and Conflict Resolution." January 1. https://www.qatar-tribune.com/article/100328/front/qatar-emerges-as-global-destination-for-mediation-dispute-resolution#google_vignette (in Arabic).

Smith, H. 2007. "Humanitarian Diplomacy: Theory and Practice." In *Humanitarian Diplomacy: Practitioners and Their Craft*. Tokyo: United Nations University Press.

UN Document. 2026. "United Humanity: Common Responsibility, Report of the UN Secretary General in Connection with the World Humanitarian Summit." February 2. UN Document A/70/709.

5 The Shift in Response of International Actors to Contemporary Security Threats and Challenges in the Case of the European Union

Beata Piskorska

Introduction

In an increasingly interconnected world, global threats and challenges have become more complex, requiring agile and coordinated responses from international actors, including local ownership, civil society organisation (CSOs), and non-governmental organisations (NGOs). These CSOs and NGOs aim at empowering their communities by responding to various needs of their people at the grassroots level. This includes decision-making authority, resource allocation, and implementation of strategies. The European Union (EU), as a major global actor, is facing a pivotal moment in which its diplomatic approaches and strategies are being tested against new and evolving global threats.

The dramatic events of the past years, between the COVID-19 pandemic, climate change, and the militarisation of international relations (IRs), including Russia–Ukraine war in Ukraine, have violently catapulted the EU into the phase of post-globalization and forced the return of strong empires in IRs. These challenges mean a completely new international phenomenon. The pandemic and a conflict are radically reorienting most IR actors' view of globalisation that not only leads to a new definition of IR but also enables to discover new and profound dynamics in the processes of the international system. Following the abovementioned challenges and threats, the EU naturally forced to shift its approach to foreign policy. As a result, the EU has increased its engagement with civil society organisations in the global south and currently in Ukraine, thus contributing to strengthening good governance. At the same time, the European Union stresses that good governance cannot be achieved without a strong and independent civil society. Therefore, in the changing European security situation, it is important to analyse the role of the EU in supporting civil society to promote good governance. This is a crucial issue; especially as the civil society is under increasing pressure worldwide at a time when the normative role of the EU is often questioned.

DOI: 10.4324/9781003565048-5

This chapter examines particularly how the EU's diplomatic strategy has changed in response to contemporary global threats, mainly in terms of security and the role of this actor in shaping these responses. First and foremost, Russian invasion of Ukraine is a turning point for European Union, mostly in its current role as a diplomatic, normative, soft power actor, specifying its security and defence policy. Moreover, the attacks against Israel and the subsequent war in Gaza in October 2023 arose just beyond the Russian attack on Ukraine in February 2022, displaying the turbulent external environment within which the European Union's external action is formulated (Glantz 2023).

The scale and significance of the growing militarisation in the European periphery both in the East and in the South are unexpected developments, presenting new security challenges to the EU. It means that the EU finds itself facing major security risks at the end of 2023 (Kruglashov 2023). It makes it necessary to apply to the analysis of the EU's role in IR and needs to adapt and change the mechanisms used so far by the EU to the new security circumstances. The EU is to build a new set of ambitious policies that define a major threat to peace and stability in Europe, and this is awaited. This fact has sent signals about the capacity of the EU to be a relevant actor on foreign policy, not just in diplomacy. However, despite significant progress in the field of security and defence, there is still much to be done.

Hence, there is a widespread phenomenon of an ongoing transformation of modern diplomacy, including that of the EU, towards the implementation of refugee diplomacy, humanitarian diplomacy, and security diplomacy (Batora 2003). This chapter aims to show approaches to European diplomacy and foreign and security policy in the broadest sense. Some critics argue that the EU's reliance on soft power and normative influence can be less effective in situations where hard power is necessary. The chapter reviews the evolution, the so-called shift of approaches to the role and position of the EU in IRs currently beyond the practice of diplomacy. Focusing on specific examples that contribute to understanding the transformation of European diplomacy, security, and foreign policy, EU also engages closely with the civil society as a part of their foreign policy (Youngs 2022).

It also discusses the theory of the EU perception in the IRs and generates a set of analytical hypotheses to explain the underlying factors that may influence and shape the content of the EU's external activity. Second, there is a current debate about whether or not a policy approach shift is taking place within the 'geopolitical awakening' of this organisation and to develop, after decades of effort, a more viable security and defence policy. The third section presents the study's empirical focus and identifies the variation in the quality of the EU's changes across the EU's existing foreign policy strategy (Schimmelfennig 2024). The research will draw on an analysis of political documents, including strategy documents, statements of the European Council and secondary literature, and the mechanism of the EU adaptation to the new security changes.

The European Union Perception in the International Relations

The EU crises are used to classified as failures: the Euro crisis (2009–2015), the migration (or refugee or Schengen) crisis (2015/16), and the COVID-19 pandemic (2020–2022); in each case, the crisis was triggered by an external shock to an integrated policy that first overwhelmed the most vulnerable member states and then developed into a manifest threat of disintegration. Although the crises have severely shaken the functioning of the European Union, each of them has consequently been a signal for positive change and, in fact, for adaptation to such change (Faiq 2024).

The European Union (EU) has become an embodiment of Europe's success in establishing integration and unity within its theoretical and methodical concept of its analysis as a soft, normative, civilian, and ethical power. Even though these conceptualizations differ among themselves, they share a positive view of the EU as a foreign policy actor guided by the common good and disinclined to use military power (Pardo 2012). Reflecting upon the historical contexts of the European region related to how identity is established as a prominent role in their interplay and stance about politics, it has driven the EU to exercise many regional enhancements through politics, economics, social, and many other aspects.

Over time, this unique method of discourse from the EU has led to a fractured image and loopholes as to how their concept of a regional organisation is normatively unaligned with the international image. These conceptualizations do not accurately capture the foreign policy behaviour of the EU. Similar to other powers, the EU is a self-interested actor seeking to maximise its own security. Hence, the EU is a normal power, no different from other polities striving to minimise external threats to their security (Pardo 2012). The EU's decision to create the Security and Defence Policy, Strategic Autonomy, and policy of resilience serves as a case study to show that the EU is a normal power.

The earliest conceptualizations of the European Community's role in the world mentioned earlier were developed by IRs science representatives. This offered the background for the idea of 'Normative Power Europe' (NPE), first defined by Manners (2002), who further developed Duchêne's notion of 'civilian power' to describe the EU's commitment to global moral causes. The NPE concept illustrates the EU's external relations as influenced by a set of normative principles and shared beliefs that are at the core of the EU's self-understanding (Wunderlich 2020). These norms and principles are codified in various places in the *acquis commauntaire*, for example, in the Copenhagen criteria and in the EU development and assistance policy. They were also incorporated in the 2009 Lisbon Treaty (Article 21) of the amended Treaty on European Union TEU. Broadly speaking, the NPE notion is that the EU's relations with the rest of the world are shaped to advance 'democracy, the rule of law, the universality and indivisibility of human rights and fundamental freedoms, respect for human dignity, the principles of equality and solidarity, and respect for the principles of the United Nations Charter and international law' (TEU 2012).

The way the EU sees itself, therefore, has important implications for the image it wants to project to the outside world (Manners 2006). The EU regards itself as a source of peace and stability for its member states—a security community built on a strong supranational institutional and legal framework. This self-image permeates every aspect of the EU's external relations and has become part of its foreign policy identity (Manners 2002; Whitman 2013). The EU aims to diffuse its own model, thereby 'normalizing' its own legal, rules-based approach to global governance (Tocci 2016, 3). NPE adds an ethical dimension to EU foreign policy—indeed, some authors have argued that NPE is related to the wider attempt to construct a European identity in the post-Cold War. In a world dominated by states, the EU aims to establish itself by differentiation, that is as a different kind of power and a force for collective good. This is done through the promotion of universal values and shared interests and the powers of attraction and persuasion (Manners 2002). The NPE concept constructs the EU to be fundamentally different from other actors in its goals and instruments, relying on the attractiveness of its own model rather than on coercion (Manners 2002). However, it is also possible to argue that this concept reflects a lack of hard-power capabilities. In strategic terms, the EU tends to rely heavily on NATO and the United States (Tocci 2016).

Due to new crises development in the IR, an evolution beyond normative power literature is observed. There is also new literature on the EU as a pioneer in setting standards (new norms) in climate change (Wunderlich 2020) or in digital market regulation. Although normative power remains relevant, but there has been evolution from Duchene and Manners that one should be aware of and position herself within this updated landscape. A more recent book (Neuman 2019) considers whether the European Union is not 'militarising' itself into a normal power, the term referring to the idea that, unlike traditional nation states, the EU exerts its influence and power primarily through non-military means.

The concept of the EU as a 'normal power' highlights its unique approach to IRs, focusing on economic power, diplomacy, and normative influence rather than traditional military might. This model reflects the EU's identity as a union of states that prioritise peace, cooperation, and the rule of law, but it also faces limitations and challenges in a world where hard power remains significant (Neuman 2019). This concept contrasts with the traditional notions of great powers or superpowers that often rely on military force to achieve their objectives. The EU's power is based on its economic strength, diplomatic influence, and the ability to set norms and standards globally. However, global perception of the EU's role as a 'normal power' can be seen as insufficient to deal with global crises, particularly in regions where military intervention is required.

This traditional identity has been challenged by current shifts in the international context and increasing geopolitical contestation. The most established approach to analysing the role of the EU in the international environment, consistent with the EU's own identity of normative authority, is strongly evaluated as Ursula von der Leyen's states:

> Commission will be a geopolitical one, attention has been paid to the changing nature of the EU towards a more geopolitical identity . . . 'in the time of the threats to our security . . . the EU must invest more in high-end defence capabilities.
>
> (Statement at the European Parliament 2024)

'Geopolitical Awakening' of the European Union Diplomacy into Security and Defence Policy

The EU's early diplomatic efforts were centred on the traditional diplomacy carried out by promoting peace and stability through economic cooperation, development aid, the enlargement policy, and the European Neighbourhood Policies. The tools of diplomatic acts were based on tools of influence such as trade agreements, development aid, and diplomatic dialogue as primary tools to influence global affairs. Therefore, in addition to what brings success to the EU in the area of diplomacy, an urgent need in the face of a worsening geopolitical context is imposing a paradigm shift on Europe, namely, the need to put security and defence at the heart of European policy. According to Josep Borell, HR/VP:

> The legacy of the Schuman Declaration was that our Union was built around the internal market and the economy . . . and this, has worked, bringing peace between the peoples of the Union. 'But for too long we have delegated our external security to the United States. We must now take strategic responsibility and become capable of defending Europe ourselves, building a strong European pillar inside NATO'.
>
> (Borrell 2024)

Former High Representative of the EU Foreign Affairs and Security Policy recommended in his statement (HR/VP blog post):

> [T]he EU needs to invest more in defence at national level. In 2023, we have spent on average 1.7% of our GDP, this percentage must increase

> to more than 2%. But, even more importantly, we need to spend more together to fill gaps, avoid duplications and increase interoperability. Only 18% of equipment purchases by our armies are currently made cooperatively. Even though we set a 35% benchmark in 2007. And since the beginning of the war against Ukraine, European armies bought 78% of new equipment from outside the EU.
>
> (Borrell 2024)

The EU as an actor in international affairs does so far have only limited experience in conflict management. The European Union as a 'Global Conflict Manager' has been involved on a limited basis in the management of various conflicts around the world, undertaking mediation facilitation, conflict resolution, and peacebuilding around the world including Afghanistan, Bosnia and Herzegovina, Cyprus, Israel–Palestine, Macedonia, and Moldova (Whitman and Wolf 2012). Nevertheless, it has formulated the goal of playing the role of a 'comprehensive' conflict manager already in 2013. In the post-Soviet region, the Union until recently hardly lived up to that ambition and has mostly restricted itself to a technical profile. Russia's 2022 invasion of Ukraine led the European Union (EU) to achieve an increased unity behind the goal of enhancing its resilience in relation to the range of geopolitical threats posed by Russia. This has involved, on the one hand, showing an increased support for Ukraine and Moldova's European integration paths and launching the European Union Advisory Mission for Civilian Security Sector Reform Ukraine (EUAM Ukraine) (Council of the European Union 2022), while, on the other, deepening integration between the members states in defence and security.

A fundamental change in the EU's approach—what we will call here the EU's 'geopolitical awakening'—finally occurred when President Putin ordered a full-scale invasion of Ukraine in February 2022. This ended the post-Cold War European security order and shattered old illusions in Germany, France, and other Western European countries about Russia's true intentions in the so-called 'shared neighbourhood'. The Kremlin's imperialist ambitions were recognised as a major threat to security and democracy in wider Europe (Raik et al. 2024).

Russia's unprovoked and illegal aggression united EU member states, in close coordination with the United States and other like-minded countries, to adopt strong and unprecedented measures to support Ukraine and impose a cost on the aggressor. The EU's new approach included the decision, explicitly formulated as a geopolitical one, to grant Ukraine a membership perspective (Raik et al. 2024).

As a result of Russia's full-scale invasion of Ukraine, the EU entered the competition as an emerging geopolitical actor in three important respects: engaging in a conflict over the European order, bringing in and strengthening its (still limited) hard power, and extending its geographical borders while these are being violently contested. Most importantly, the EU is actively trying to shape the future of the European order that was challenged by Russia's war against Ukraine. Furthermore, by granting candidate country status to Ukraine, it took a clear stance on its future borders, while these were violently contested (Raik et al. 2024).

At the same time, there are key differences between Russian and EU approaches to geopolitical competition: the EU's vision of order remains rooted in rules and international law, which have been grossly violated by Russia; the EU does not violently impose its so-called 'liberal empire' on other actors; and it continues to reject the very idea of spheres of influence. Geopolitics is concerned with the impact of geographical factors on IRs. The study of geopolitics has often been viewed as a 'branch of the realist tradition' (Guzzini 2012), although in the 1990s and 2000s, there was a popular strand of 'critical geopolitics' that applied constructivist theory. To remain relevant in the world of geopolitical competition, it has been widely argued that the EU must adapt. But hardly anyone calling for a geopolitical EU means that it should (or could) mirror Russian efforts to impose its sphere of influence by force and deny the sovereign rights of its neighbours. The geopolitics practised by the EU is different from the realist geopolitics practised by Russia, which raises the question of whether it is justified to call it 'geopolitics' at all.

In the history of European integration on the way to the signing of the Maastricht Treaty and its ratification by European leaders, there have been constant discussions on security issues. These included the enhancement of the EU's role and position in regional and global security and its accountability to member states. The EU promoted the idea of a political union responsible for the common foreign and defence policy of the member states. These ideas were identified as one of the three new pillars built in the Maastricht Treaty. At the same time, this pillar embraced the idea and mechanism of intergovernmentalism rather than supranationalism in security and foreign policymaking. In this regard, these innovations spark further discussions about some issues, including the extent to which the EU has to develop a capacity to be an international actor in the field of foreign and security policy.

A huge challenge for the EU in terms of the expectations of transforming diplomacy is to maintain, or indeed achieve, full internal coherence in maintaining a unified position among EU member states on security and defence issues. Second, it is to verify the effectiveness of strategic autonomy, its feasibility, and desirability in the face of global power shifts. Third and finally, the question of balancing its normative power with the need to engage in realpolitik in an increasingly multipolar world is a big challenge.

It was only a series of crises that forced the EU to accelerate the existing objectives and revise its foreign and security strategy. However, it seems that previous efforts to make the EU more consolidated on security issues have ultimately failed, and the EU is particularly hesitant when discussing US leadership in the areas of responsibility of two important international organisations: NATO and the EU in Europe. Different concerns and visions of

European security and the global conflict prevention agenda have contributed to a kind of redistribution of powers and competences between NATO and the EU. So far, NATO remains the most important actor on hard security issues, while the EU focuses mainly on the soft security agenda, including arms trafficking, prevention and resolution of regional and sub-regional conflicts, etc.

This compromise was reached in the late 1990s. It serves as a reference point for the development and implementation of other attempts to make the EU a true global actor. While the EU initially viewed these crises with a sense of surprise and anxiety, it used them as a window of opportunity to push forward the existing goals and revise its strategy. These crises were framed by the EU as threats and challenges (and evidence of the world order becoming increasingly uncertain) from which it had to safeguard itself and become resilient (Håkansson 2023). The EU's assessment of the causes and impact of crises led it to gradually embrace the concept of geopolitics and adopt the need to enhance its resilience as a centrepiece of its strategy in external relations. Federica Morgherini, former High Representative of the EU, also emphasised that not taking advantage of the opportunity offered by external crises would lead 'to the foreign policy of isolation, fear, protectionism and confrontation, and this is the European way' (Mogherini 2019). More particularly, the decade of crises offered a chance for the EU to enhance its military capabilities.

Referring to the global consequences caused by the conflicts in international environment—Russia–Ukraine war and the Israeli–Palestinian war carry regional externalities, including a clash of ideologies, in particular through Russia's contestation of European integration itself and the actions taken by the organisation. Moreover, these developments will lead to economic linkages and political instability that could lead to a collapse of the geopolitical landscape in the European region. Considering the case of Russia's invasion of Ukraine, the robust external threat from Russia causes a general increase in European identity, especially among EU member states, as heterogeneity in the region implies that the intensity caused by the conflict is differentiated. Resulting from the parameters of EU identity, economic perceptions, political support, and branches of alternative levels of identity that are explored by the Ukraine–Russia conflict have conflated proximity with power dynamics in Eastern Europe, as reflected in the conflict in the review of the EU and European countries that are actively involved in the Ukraine–Russia conflict (Gehring 2022).

Given the international assessment of the current state of the EU, what strategies can the EU adopt to play a proactive role in resolving global geopolitical tensions and promoting multilateral solutions? There is no doubt that the European Union needs to move beyond familiar complaints about the lack of a common strategic culture and EU encroachment on NATO responsibilities. Geostrategic and economic imperatives dictate that the EU should develop its foreign and security policy beyond civilian crisis management in the EU neighbourhood and military training and security sector reform. Clarity of purpose, coherence, enhanced EU capabilities compatible with those implemented by NATO has created a Strategic Compass oriented towards building European strategic autonomy in a way that strengthens European defence.

More Security than Diplomacy—Strategy of Resilience

One can distinguish between several levels of EU evolution of diplomacy towards security threats triggered by the Russia–Ukraine conflict. One of them is abandoning the tactics of denying geopolitical competition with Russia on February 24, 2022. For the first time, the EU clearly chose the side of Ukraine in the Russia–Ukraine conflict, and mobilised strong support was arguably a significant shift towards the EU becoming a geopolitical actor in contrast to its usual role of a mediator and facilitator in external conflicts.

The EU has also used predominantly its existing regulatory powers, rules, and decision-making mechanisms, for example for sanctions against Russia and Belarus, the international protection of refugees, and the facilitation of imports from Ukraine. In addition, the member states redirected and topped up existing resources, mainly the European Peace Facility (EPF) established in 2021 and funded by extra-budgetary member state contributions, to support Ukraine militarily. In October 2022, the EU agreed on a novel EU Military Assistance Mission (EUMAM), but the actual training of Ukrainian armed forces takes place in the member states. Finally, the EU did not move to abolish the Council's unanimity rule in matters of foreign and security policy (Council of the EU 2022).

Unprecedented restrictive measures have also been a core element of the EU's response to Russian aggression. The EU had already imposed a range of economic restrictions on Russia, including both sectoral and individual measures, in response to its annexation of Crimea in 2014 and its role in the conflict in eastern Ukraine, which the EU avoided calling a 'war'. The sanctions were extensively reviewed and extended in 2022 in response to the 'unprovoked and unjustified military aggression against Ukraine'

(Council of the EU 2022, 2023). Even though the war in Ukraine does not constitute a direct military attack on the EU, it goes against the integrity of an EU-associated country, the expansion of the EU regulatory space, and the liberal–democratic values of the EU. Russian autocratic imperialism clashes with the EU's liberal supranational order. Moreover, it raised fears that the restoration of Russia's sphere of influence would not stop with Ukraine (Schimmelfennig 2024). None of the attacks resulted from failures of integrated policies. The EU's Neighbourhood and Eastern Partnership policies had gradually paved the way for the association of Ukraine and other Eastern European countries.

The latter evolution has seen, for example, enhanced coordination in the areas of military procurement, as well as the development of what can be seen as a new security strategy for the EU—that is the Strategic Compass. However, these developments have progressively built on a major revision of the

EU's strategy in world politics that occurred in the latter part of the 2010s—which has come to be seen as the 'resilience turn' (Korosteleva 2020b). This salient transformation saw the concept of resilience being included as a centrepiece of EU strategy.

The concept offered a simple solution to the range of crises that the EU experienced at the time, ranging from the Euro crisis, the migrant crisis to the Ukraine crisis (starting with 2014). In its simple form, resilience has been defined by the EU as the ability to predict, manage, and overcome risks—in the case of world politics, geopolitical risks, and challenges. Thus, the EU has prioritised the need to enhance resilience as a key way of adapting to a changing world order, that was perceived to be increasingly dominated by geopolitics and averse to EU leadership (Nitoiu and Pasatoiu 2020). The adoption of resilience as a centrepiece of EU strategy has informed a series of debates in the literature, which focus on the nature and extent of this transformation, with scholars primarily debating the existence of a critical juncture in European integration and whether it has led to paradigmatic change or the adaption of a state of business as usual (Korosteleva 2020a).

Federica Morgherini recognised the window opportunity to embrace resilience as a pathway for the EU to deal with the decade of crises:

> [L]ooking beyond the crises of the moment, and working to prevent the next crisis, or to stabilise countries that are coming out of a conflict and that risk to fall back again into a crisis mode, if you do not invest to stabilise them properly. We put the concept of resilience at the centre of our work.
>
> (Mogherini 2019)

For much of the post-Cold War period, the EU had been operating based on the assumption that it represents a different type of international actor that managed to overcome structural geopolitical constraints. The very development of the EU and the model of regional integration and global governance it created were framed as an alternative way of constructing the world order (in opposition to the centrality of nation states).

The EU' s Role in Supporting Civil Society Organizations in Conflict Areas

The EU has played an important role in supporting the civil society for many years. Its aim is to promote good governance in member states and neighbouring countries. Since the beginning of Russia's full-scale invasion, the European Union has stood by Ukraine and provided comprehensive military, humanitarian, and financial support, including support for Ukrainian civil society organisations and media. The European Union also focuses on supporting and developing independent media at all levels—from national to local, because, as aptly defined, they are the watchdogs of democracy and the voice of civil society. Their role as carriers of reliable information is particularly noticeable in the challenging times of hybrid aggression, which is widely waged on the information front (Moving Forward Together 2024b).

The EU has undertaken a number of urgent decisions, including by redirecting funding for existing projects to meet Ukraine's immediate needs, including assistance to civil society organisations (CSOs) and the media, while still maintaining their ability to protect human rights, protect socially vulnerable groups, enhance the accountability of public authorities, and promote reforms aimed at integration with the EU.

In response to the challenges imposed by the war, the EU launched together with the Black Sea Trust for Regional Cooperation (BST), a project of the German Marshall Fund proposals that aims to support Ukrainian civil society organisations (CSOs) in order to mitigate the immediate and the medium- to long-term impact of the Russia–Ukraine war (Moving Forward Together 2024a).

The same EU then calls for Emergency Support to civil society and media in response to the Ukraine war and, in partnership with ERIM (Equal Rights Independent Media) funded projects, aims to strengthen the resilience and effectiveness of war-affected CSOs and civil society actors and address priorities such as: capacity building and emergency support to relocated CSOs and independent media outlets to allow them to continue their work, including training, establishing medium- to long-term strategies and programmes, improving office rent, purchasing equipment, etc.; relocation support from war-torn to safe regions within Ukraine, including transportation, temporary accommodation, health, psychosocial/anti-trauma services; and assistance to internally displaced people in accordance with their needs, including health, employment, psychosocial/anti-trauma, education, etc. The services provided, however, will not include humanitarian support (Ibid). As of today, the European Union also funds a number of grant projects with a total budget of €28 million to support Ukrainian media and journalists. In particular, these projects provide financial assistance for the functioning of Ukrainian media, the safety of journalists, the fight against disinformation, psychological media operations, and manipulations (EUNeighboursEast 2024). That is why the European Union supports mass media and journalists in Ukraine in the face of current challenges and threats. Over the past few years, over 150 media of various levels have received financial assistance from the EU in the amount of more than EUR 15 million.

Building more resilient democracies with the help of citizens and civil society organisations is at the core of a new recommendation of the European Commission. The EU calls Member States to promote the participation of citizens and civil society organisations in public policymaking. This could improve the quality of decision-making processes and renew trust in democracy. A strengthened civil society is a key element of any democratic system and is an asset in its own right. 'Supporting and involving civil society in all its diversity is therefore an essential part of EU external relations' (European Commission 2023).

The EU has supported the Georgian and Ukrainian civil societies since the very beginning of their development both financially and politically by defending and promoting the key role it plays in a democratic society (EEAS 2021). The EU's goal remains to enhance the sustainability and accountability of CSOs as well as to ensure an enabling environment, improved policy dialogue between civil society and public institutions (especially with regard to budgetary and legislative processes), and stronger civic participation in all regions of Georgia. EU support also aims at developing the civil society's capacity to be involved in all sectors covered by the political agenda (EEAS 2021).

The importance of civil society in Ukraine is growing, especially in wartimes. Civil society organisations need further support in increasing their capacities and in developing capabilities in funding diversification, not-for-profit management, transparency, and accountability as well as communication and constituencies' building. Therefore, the EU initiated as well a project titled 'Support to EU engagement with civil society organisations in Ukraine II'. Within the project, a team of experts is working with the civil society team in the EU Delegation and EU grantees to increase the impact of EU support to CSOs, including through numerous communication activities (EU Neighbours East 2022).

The EU Strategic Compass

The EU's approach to security and stability has changed noticeably in the EU Strategic Compass (SC) adopted in March 2022, which states that the European security has become a field of strategic rivalry and a contested domain in which some countries' behaviour is driven by historical rights and spheres of influence rather than [by] adherence to internationally agreed principles and rules. At the time the war in Ukraine started, the EU was also on the verge of adopting its new Strategic Compass in Security and Defence after a two-year development process (EEAS 2022).

The project aims to set the course for the EU's security and defence ambitions for the rest of this decade and beyond. It will include all states willing and able to participate in activities involving capability integration, fully compatible with and within the framework of European NATO. Illustrating that the EU has started to regard stability and security as important areas of its development, the Compass points to a changing EU identity. Thus, alongside its long-standing normative identity, expressed as 'norm initiator' and 'norm defender' (Gstöhl and Schunz 2021), we are currently witnessing the emergence of a more geopolitical identity. The SC is a new take on an old problem: trying to imbue the EU with strategic actorness and autonomy. It exists within an institutional set-up, but one which at present is concerned with declaratory diplomacy rather than solving real-world problems that require capabilities, resources, and commitment.

The EU as a Defender of Multilateralism

The European Union still is the main defender of multilateralism, and its attempts to enrich multilateralism hold keys for international cooperation. The EU's role as an international actor is deeply ingrained in its identity, as driven by this commitment to multilateralism, with EU documents and treaties incorporating multilateralism as a key priority (O'Sullivan 2021). The European Parliament also clearly states this mission:

> Multilateralism is the only guarantee for peace, security, and sustainable and inclusive development in a highly polarised international environment . . . is at the heart of the European Union's approach to its CFSP as enshrined in the TEU . . . and stresses . . . the importance of teaming up with like-minded EU strategic partners, in particular NATO and emerging countries in order to defend the global rule-based order that is founded on international and humanitarian law and multilateral treaties; recalls that the EU's CFSP is based on partnership and multilateralism.
>
> (European Parliament 2020)

The EU actively engaged in diplomatic initiatives to help resolve the conflict and promote dialogue between Russia and Ukraine. As a way of multilateralising conflict management in the post-Soviet space, the EU has supported and worked with the Organisation for Security and Cooperation in Europe as the main pan-European security structure. The EU was also supportive of the Normandy format that was active from June 2014 to February 2022 and which revolved around the delegation of diplomatic efforts to Germany and France (Lohsen and Morcos 2022). It supported the Normandy Format talks, which involved Ukraine, Russia, Germany, and France, and aimed to find a peaceful solution to the conflict. The EU also endorsed the Minsk Agreements, which outlined a roadmap for a ceasefire and a political settlement in eastern Ukraine.

Conclusion

The EU's shift in diplomatic and security strategies reflects its efforts to adapt to a rapidly changing global security environment, though challenges remain in achieving a cohesive and effective approach. This undoubtedly makes implications for the EU's evolving role in global security and stability, particularly in its interactions with other major powers. However, the EU still stands at a crossroads, where its decisions in the coming years will determine its role and influence in the global order amidst growing security threats.

The EU pays significant attention to helping Ukrainian CSOs, especially now, when the country is fighting against the Russian aggressor for the very existence of Ukraine and its democratic European future. Civil society is a key partner for the EU in delivering a sustainable impact for communities through EU external action.

In the Russia–Ukraine war, the EU has also used predominantly its existing regulatory powers, rules, and decision-making mechanisms, for example, for sanctions against Russia and Belarus, the international protection of refugees, and the facilitation of imports from Ukraine. In addition, the member states redirected and topped up existing resources, mainly the European Peace Facility (EPF) established in 2021 and funded by extra-budgetary member state contributions, to support Ukraine militarily. In October 2022, the EU agreed on a novel EU Military Assistance Mission (EUMAM), but the actual training of Ukrainian armed forces takes place in the member states. Finally, the EU did not move to abolish the Council's unanimity rule in matters of foreign and security policy.

Undoubtedly, the Russian invasion of Ukraine was a historical turning point that has forced the EU to become an actor in the biggest geopolitical conflict in Europe since World War II. The full-scale invasion pushed the EU to take the side of Ukraine and tackle the conflict as an emerging geopolitical actor in its own right, engaging along the three dimensions of order, hard power, and borders. The EU pursued its goals in the geopolitical competition predominantly through civilian means, but it also took significant steps towards strengthening its hard-power capabilities and contributing military assistance. Furthermore, by granting candidate country status to Ukraine, it took a clear stance on the EU's future borders, while these were being contested by the Russian aggression. At the same time, however, the EU did not engage in geopolitics on the same terms as Russia—it was defending its vision of European order and Ukraine's determination to be part of this order, without imposing it (Raik et al. 2024). Thus, from the EU's perspective, the geopolitical competition also involved a strong element of values and norms. The nature of the EU's response, including its emphasis on values and its limited hard power, raises the question whether 'geopolitics' is the most appropriate concept to characterise the EU's response.

The changing security environment in the neighbourhood of the European Union allows the identification of three strategic changes for the next decade. These have the potential to fundamentally change the way the European Union perceives and shapes its place in the world: first, a shift towards a 'multipolar world', characterised by a period in which rules are more contested and relative power between states plays a greater role in shaping international affairs; second, a shift from economics to security—a shift in which economic relations are reassessed in the light of increased military competition in a more secure and less stable world; and, finally, a shift from effectively executed diplomacy to resilience—a shift in the drivers of economic behaviour whereby building greater resilience and addressing pressing social and sustainability issues become more prominent.

References

Batora, J. 2003. "Does the European Union Transform the Institution of Diplomacy." Discussion Papers in Diplomacy 87. https://www.clingendael.org/sites/default/files/2016-02/20030700_cli_paper_dip_issue87.pdf

Borrell, J. 2024. "Europe Day 2024: The Need of a Paradigm Shifts for the EU." https://www.eeas.europa.eu/eeas/europe-day-2024-need-paradigm-shift-eu_en

Consolidated Version of the Treaty of the European Union (TEU). 2012. "Official Journal of the European Union C326/15." https://eur-lex.europa.eu/resource.html?uri=cellar:2bf140bf-a3f8-4ab2-b506-fd71826e6da6.0023.02/DOC_1&format=PDF

Council of the European Union. 2022. "Council Decision (CFSP) 2022/452 of 18 March 2022 Amending Decision 2014/486/CFSP on the European Union Advisory Mission for Civilian Security Sector Reform Ukraine (EUAM Ukraine)." https://eur-lex.europa.eu/legal-content/EN/TXT/?uri=CELEX%3A32022D0452

Council of the EU. 2023. "EU Restrictive Measures against Russia over Ukraine (Since 2014)." Accessed September 2023. https://www.consilium.europa.eu/en/policies/sanctions/restrictive-measures-against-russia-over-ukraine

EEAS. 2021. "EU Roadmap for Engagement with Civil Society in Georgia 2018–2024 (Updated in 2021)." https://www.eeas.europa.eu/sites/default/files/documents/cs-roadmap-2021-24-inal.pdf

EEAS. 2022. "A Strategic Compass for Security and Defence: For a European Union That Protects Its Citizens, Values and Interests and Contributes to International Peace and Security." https://www.eeas.europa.eu/sites/default/files/documents/strategic_compass_en3_web.Pdf

EU Neighbours East. 2022. "Support to EU Engagement with Civil Society Organisations in Ukraine II." https://euneighbourseast.eu/projects/eu-project-page/?id=1681

EU Neighbours East. 2024. "EU Launches New Communication Campaign to Showcase Its Support to Ukrainian Civil Society and Media." https://euneighbourseast.eu/news/latest-news/eu-launches-new-communication-campaign-to-showcase-its-support-to-ukrainian-civil-society-and-media/

European Commission. 2023. "Recommendation on the Participation of Citizens and Civil Society Organisations in Public Policy-making, General Publications, C(2023) 8627 final 12 December 2023." https://eur-lex.europa.eu/legal-content/EN/TXT/PDF/?uri=PI_COM:C(2023)8627

European Parliament. 2020. "Resolution of a6 July 2022 on the EU and the Defence of Multilateralism." https://www.europarl.europa.eu/doceo/document/TA-9-2022-0286_EN.html

Faiq, R., ed. 2024. "European Identity and the 21st Century European Union: Steering the Political Project." http://moderndiplomacy.eu/2024/06/17/european-identity-and-the-21st-century-eu-steering-the-political-project/

Gehring, K. 2022. "Can External Threats Foster a European Union Identity? Evidence from Russia's Invasion of Ukraine." *The Economic Journal* 132 (644): 1489–516. https://doi.org/10.1093/ej/ueab088

Glantz, M. 2023. *How Does the Israel-Hamas War Impact Russia and Ukraine? The Middle East Conflict Adds Another Layer of Complexity to Both Sides'*

Effort to Court Global Support and to Washington's Effort to Aid Kyiv. United States Institute for Peace. https://www.usip.org/publications/2023/11/how-does-israel-hamas-war-impact-russia-and-ukraine

Gstöhl, S., and S. Schunz. 2021. *The External Action of the European Union. Concepts, Approaches, Theories*. Bloomsbury Publishing.

Guzzini, S. 2012. "Which Geopolitics?" In *The Return of Geopolitics in Europe? Social Mechanisms and Foreign Policy Identity Crises*, edited by Stefano Guzzini. Cambridge University Press

Håkansson, H. 2023. "The Strengthened Role of the European Union in Defence: The Case of the Military Mobility Project." *Defence Studies Volume* 23 (3): 436–56. https://doi.org/10.1080/14702436.2023.2213647

Korosteleva, E. A. 2020a. "Paradigmatic or Critical? Resilience as a New Turn in EU Governance for the Neighbourhood." *Journal of International Relations and Development* 23 (3): 682–700.

Korosteleva, E. A. 2020b. "Reclaiming Resilience Back: A Local Turn in EU External Governance." *Contemporary Security Policy* 41 (2).

Kruglashov, A. 2023. "The Reaction of International Organizations to Global Security Challenges." In *Global Public Goods and Sustainable Development in the Practice of International Organizations. Responding to Challenges of Today's World*, edited by Ewa Latoszek and A. Kłos, 74. Brill.

Lohsen A., and P. Morcos. 2022. "Understanding the Normandy Format and Its Relation to the Current Standoff with Russia." https://www.csis.org/analysis/understanding-normandy-format-and-its-relation-current-standoff-russia

Manners, I. 2002. "Normative Power: A Contradiction in Terms?" *Journal of Common Market Studies* 40 (2).

Manners, I. 2006. "Normative Power Europe Reconsidered: Beyond the Crossroads." *Journal of European Public Policy* 13.

Mogherini, F. 2019. "Speech by High Representative/Vice-president Federica Mogherini on "The EU's Role as a Global Player for Peace and Stability" at Oxford University." https://www.eeas.europa.eu/eeas/speech-high-representativevice-president-federica-mogherini-%E2%80%9C-eu%E2%80%99s-role-global-player-peace_en?s=136

Moving Forward Together. 2024a. "Emergency Support to Civil Society and Media in Response to the Ukraine War." https://www.gmfus.org/emergency-support-civil-society-and-media-response-ukraine-war

Moving Forward Together. 2024b. "The EU Supports Civil Society and Each of Us." https://eu4ukraine.eu/en/whats-happening-en/campaigns-en/together-we-act-en/together-we-act.html

Neuman, M., ed. 2019. "Democracy Promotion and the Normative Power Europe Framework." In *The European Union in South Eastern Europe, Eastern Europe, and Central Asia*. Springer, 8.

Nitoiu, C., and F. Pasatoiu. 2020. "Hybrid Geopolitics in EU-Russia Relations: Understanding the Persistence of Conflict and Cooperation." *East European Politics* 36 (4): 499–511.

O'Sullivan, D. 2021. *The European Union and the Multilateral System. Lessons from Past Experience and Future Challenges*. Briefing. The EU System in Perspective. https://www.europarl.europa.eu/RegData/etudes/BRIE/2021/689365/EPRS_BRI(2021)689365_EN.pdf

Pardo, P. R. 2012. "Normal Power Europe: Non-Proliferation and the Normalization of EU's Foreign Policy." *Journal of European Integration* 34 (1): 1–18.

Raik, K., S. Blockmans, A. Osypchuk, and A. Suslov. 2024. "EU Policy towards Ukraine: Entering Geopolitical Competition over European Order." *International Spectator* 59 (1): 39–58.

Schimmelfennig, F. 2024. "Crisis and Polity Formation in the European Union." *Journal of European Public Policy* 31 (10): 1–2.

Statement at the European Parliament Plenary by President Ursula von der Leyen, Candidate for a Second Mandate 2024–2029. 2024. "Strasbourg." https://ec.europa.eu/commission/presscorner/detail/en/statement_24_3871

Tocci, N. 2016. "The Making of the EU Global Strategy." *Contemporary Security Policy* 37 (3): 461–72. https://doi.org/10.1080/13523260.2016.1232559

Whitman, R. G. 2013. "The Neo-Normative Turn in Theorising the EU's International Presence." *Cooperation and Conflict* 48 (2): 171–93. https://doi.org/10.1177/0010836713485538

Whitman, R. G., and S. Wolff. 2012. *The European Union as a Global Conflict Manager*, 272. Taylor & Francis.

Wunderlich, J.-U. 2020. "Positioning as Normative Actors: China and the EU in Climate Change Negotiations." *Journal of Common Market Studies* 58 (5): 1107–23.

Youngs, R. 2022. "EU Support to Civil Society and Good Governance. Trends and Challenges." *Aktuelle Analysen* No. 92. https://www.hss.de/download/publications/AA_92_EU-Unterstuetzung_englisch.pdf

6 Challenges to Local Human Rights Defenders and Community Peacebuilders in Libya

Ibrahim Natil

Introduction

Five militants murdered Salwa Bugaighis, a co-founder of the Libyan Women's Platform for Peace (LWPP), at her home on June 25, 2014. LWPP was launched by over 30 women from various social, political, and cultural backgrounds and locations across Libya in October 2011. Salwa worked until the last hour of her life to mobilise people to participate peacefully in the democratic process by voting to ensure a peaceful transition for power post-Qaddafi. Violence had increased against women's rights and peacebuilding movements, and Fariha al-Berkawi, a member of the first parliament (General National Congress, GNC), was assassinated in Derna on July 17, 2014. Ms Siham Sergiwa, a member of Libya's House of Representatives in Benghazi, disappeared on July 17, 2019. Hanan al-Barassi, a political and human rights defender, was assassinated on November 10, 2020. LWPP's leaders, friends, colleagues, and volunteers have since been working to bring the killers to justice (Libyan Women's Platform for Peace 2023).

Assassination of Salwa Bugaighis is a threat for all women who engage in their societies. Jad (2018) discusses actively women's participation in collective public activities to try to shape their own future in the context of violence and colonisation. The power of participatory civil society is reflected to meet the vision of engaging women in civic actions and freedom of expression despite the absence of peace. Their narratives and roles also contribute to introducing long-term changes in attitudes, stereotypes, and prejudices and promoting women's rights, fostering tolerance and understanding of the 'other' by applying lessons learnt from other conflicts in the world (Paffenholz and Spurk 2010, 66–76). Women, however, may view their representation as an outcome of empowerment according to the cultural context of their society.

The latest military attacks on civil society organisations (CSOs) happened after the Israeli occupation forces raided the offices of six leading Palestinian civil society and human rights organisations in Ramallah, an occupied

DOI: 10.4324/9781003565048-6

city in the West Bank, on August 18, 2022. These organisations had been labelled 'terrorists' by Israel in October 2021 and accused of connections to the Popular Front for the Liberation of Palestine (PFLP). One of these organisations is the Union of Palestinian Women Committees (UPWC), funded by international donors, European organisations in particular. UPWC is a key pillar of wider Palestinian civil society in delivering social and economic development services for Palestinians who live in the occupied territories.

Young women and their CSOs' contributions to decision-making processes in terms of 'local peacebuilding' are still far from finding engagement or influence, as discussed by Berents and McEvoy-Levy (2015). This also includes the examination of women's CSOs in the post-conflict approach by exploring the barriers challenging women's CSOs in reference to the 'local ownership' of peacebuilding and community development actions. Case studies from Libya were selected to discuss these issues as the significance of the relationship between women's CSOs and their leaders' impact on local peacebuilding, community development, and change processes should be considered (McEvoy-Levy 2006; Ozerdem and Podder 2015).

The complex issues of local peacebuilding, such as women's memory, truth, and silence, should be given further consideration, as Porter (2007) discusses. These issues would strengthen the base of contribution for peacebuilding and change through enhancing engagement in empowerment activities. This would, in turn, promote the understanding of the key elements of local ownership and peacebuilding. Local CSOs, such as the Libyan Women's Platform for Peace (LWPP), have implemented community activities to engage and empower a large number of young women on the values, concepts, and practices of local peacebuilding. To what extent have CSOs succeeded in delivering peacebuilding activities in spite of financial, social, and political constraints? The complications of understanding the local ownership and foreign aid and their impact on local peacebuilding processes are discussed in this chapter. Local ownership is a problem for international partners, such as the EU and the UN, as Bojicic-Dzelilovic and Martin (2016) discuss. These issues have already imposed considerable barriers on women's CSOs today, including community engagement, contributions to local peacebuilding, human rights, and community development.

To enrich the examination of women's CSOs and their contribution to local peacebuilding, the author also interviewed local CSO activists and was allowed access to the data of a local CSO to study their contributions to peacebuilding. This chapter also analyses some CSOs' activities, work delivered, statements, and literature produced by their representatives and activists from Libya. Therefore, it uses the case study approach to examine the challenges and shifts facing CSOs in different cultural contexts, political environments, and social dynamics. Gerring's (2011) case study approach is used to understand these differences within the subfield of comparative politics. This approach assists in understanding these countries, which have been enduring very severe circumstances owing to economic deterioration, the absence of reconciliation, violence, and divisions. These circumstances have already created barriers to CSOs' operations and deliveries.

This chapter also discusses the challenges facing local women's CSOs and their activists and defenders in contributing to local peacebuilding. What are the local challenges facing women's CSOs? How can they overcome them? Who engages in overcoming them? Who is responsible for engaging with the local community? What is the impact of CSOs' engagement on the local peacebuilding processes? To what extent do these CSOs understand the concept and practice of local peacebuilding? Is the local peacebuilding concept a part of CSOs' missions, visions, and activities? Do they use the concept of local peacebuilding to please the donors? Is there any relationship between the local ownership and CSOs' participatory approach? This chapter also reviews the existing literature to define the 'local ownership of peacebuilding' and contributions to community development and human rights activities since CSOs' grassroots activities may empower local people's contributions to decision-making processes in terms of peacebuilding and local ownership post-conflict consensus-building (Donais 2012).

Local Ownership of Peacebuilding Networks and Structures

This consensus and understanding may give local women's organisations, leaders, and activists a platform to decide on societal changes despite conflicts, a lack of policies, restrictive political environments, and the complexity of the sociocultural and economic contexts. CSOs attempt to challenge these social, economic, and political constraints and circumstances by institutionalising programmes to facilitate women's active participation in peacebuilding activities in partnership with international donors, such as the UN and the EU. The guiding policies of CSOs' intervention at the local level rely on effective cooperation and partnership as a key to programmes' implementation (Paffenholz 2010). This will assist the reader to understand women's role as agents for peacebuilding in their societies (Ozerdem and Podder 2015).

This chapter also considers the power of the leadership of young women in CSOs and their impact on local networks in implementing community actions and campaigns to contribute to peace, security, and development (Pruitt and Lee-Koo 2020). This can be seen through CSOs' effective engagement with local networks or building new coalitions to promote the local ownership of implementing peacebuilding activities to introduce change (Natil 2016, 2019, 2020a). The role of local people in peacebuilding is also discussed. Previously, Ozerdem and Podder (2015) considered young people, including women, in conflict and peacebuilding theoretically by highlighting the ways in which they are overlooked in peacebuilding and considering their agential capacity to contribute. Young women aged 17 to 35 are a significant part of society, having a serious influence in times of both peace and conflict, yet they are not included in peacebuilding programmes at the leadership or policy level. The foundations of this space and peacebuilding have already been discussed by McEvoy-Levy (2006).

Local ownership of peacebuilding, however, has been a serious matter for local women's CSOs in contributing to the empowerment of their communities. CSOs such as LWPP coordinate and cooperate with community centres from different areas of Libya in order to empower young women aged 17 to 35 in the values, concepts, and practices of local peacebuilding through programmes of leadership, campaigning, and voluntary and advocacy work (Natil, 2014, 2019, 2020b). Young women activists succeeded in benefitting from these local structural activities to enhance their active listening and mediation roles to solve their family's social problems (Natil 2020b). These structures also give a specific space for young women leaders to raise issues of gender to distinguish between their contributions to conflict, peacebuilding, and security (Pruitt and Lee-Koo 2020). LWPP also succeeded in launching a six-month project in Libya to train a group of female mediators:

> Entitled "wasitat" (women mediators), the campaign Introduced examples of active participation by women In successful mediation processes In Libya In the past and presents. The peace building experiences of 10 female mediators from Benghazi, Zwara, Sabha, El Baida, Taourgha, Tripoli, Zawia, and Janzour were under-scored in a live radio talk program. Video interviews highlighted 13 mediators, while 40 posters showcased perspectives of the women mediators on women's role in reconciliation.
>
> (LWPP Web 2023)

This contribution of young women's leaders to local peacebuilding presents real challenges and achievements in highly conservative societies like Palestine and Libya, where shared values of conservatism and religion remain crucial factors in both their cultures and behaviours (Merrill 2017, 124). Some local CSOs, such as LWPP, have promoted partnerships with local actors, such as the World Organization of Al-Azhar Graduates, launching the 'Fostering Wasati Islam in the Libyan Nation' programme in December 2016. LWPP also aims at supporting the prevention of violent extremism in Libya and has discussed 'The Personal Status Law between Human Rights and Islamic Perspectives' (Libyan Women's Platform for Peace 2023).

Some CSOs like LWPP have invited open-minded religious leaders to highlight the significant role of women in local peacebuilding and community development. This also presents a new approach to civil society peacebuilding based on women's active engagement and effective contribution. This indicates the powerful role of women in a bottom-up process rather than a top-down approach through formal state institutions (Noma, Aker, and Freeman 2012, 7–32). These networks look like a participatory approach in their processes, which combine discussions, dialogue, coalition-building, campaigning, advocacy work, and various interactions between activists themselves and other stakeholders such as politicians, policymakers, and businesspeople (Paffenholz and Spurk 2010, 67).

CSOs' participatory approach, however, is hampered by domestic and political violence. In other words, their participatory approach is to engage young women in local or grassroots peacebuilding to contribute to change or development in the short term only. These networks, structures, or groups are essential for local ownership despite unstainable peace actions. The significance of these networks or structures of local young women is to make citizens more qualified or empowered (Michels and de Graaf 2010).

Designed Local Peacebuilding Programmes

These designed peacebuilding programmes are responsive to the broader violent political shifts and challenges. To what extent has women's engagement in local civil society initiatives funded by international donors increased their participation in peacebuilding processes? Considering this illustrates how young people, including women, contribute to local peacebuilding activities to change their circumstances despite the absence of peace (Natil 2019). However, vulnerable grassroots groups like women are still excluded from peacebuilding; as Porter (2007, 2) explains, they 'usually are informal, ad hoc and rarely part of formal peace processes, so their stories often drift, unacknowledged'.

These peacebuilding programmes aim to introduce societal transformation through participatory civil society approaches and informal grassroots methodologies of promoting civic engagement based on voluntary efforts, advocacy, and campaigning, solving problems and helping each other. Women's active engagement in community development and grassroots programmes is a core principle of human rights, democratisation, good governance, conflict resolution, and local peacebuilding approaches. This increases community solidarity by empowering women through engaging in community participation actions. As Arostegui (2013) argues: 'Women's empowerment has come with the education, advocacy, and organisational skills that they developed as a result of conflict—they now have women's networks and women's peace groups, which were not there previously'.

Women's groups and CSOs have already employed a number of accommodating policies and operations to increase their interventions and activism to promote the values of women's resilience and empowerment in local peacebuilding activities. Several activists, for example, help to provide vital information to tackle the issues of violence against women. These moves also include analytical examinations of the activities, efforts, and endeavours made by CSOs to achieve the various objectives of young women's engagement in local peacebuilding activities by organising public meetings, capacity-building activities, campaigning, surveying and monitoring, and advocacy and research:

> The involvement of Civil Society Organizations in the peace negotiations and national dialogue in Libya, particularly of women and youth, remain limited and virtually absent. A challenge that has steered CSOs to adapt a new approach guided by strengthening civil society cooperation across Libya, and to target horizontally a trust building approach at grassroots. At the crux of our framework at LWPP, is the view that such levels of cooperation between CSOs and local communities is critical to reposition the two vertically with political forces in Libya. This would broaden the space for a more proactive direct involvement in Libya's peacebuilding and state-building process. For us, community trust is critical to enhancing the role of CSOs as change makers in Libya.
>
> (Libyan Women's Platform for Peace 2023)

The promotion of localism and/or local ownership of grassroots engagement in peacebuilding activities, as Cho, Byrne, and Pelter explain, concerns 'individual or collective actions in which people participate to improve the well-being of communities or society in general' (2020, 6). This grassroots contribution and engagement of women's CSOs can be considered through the lenses of security, transformative change, and participation (Porter 2013). Are women's CSOs' contributions, however, considered a form of peacebuilding and a process of local ownership? In spite of international financial donations, CSOs' peacebuilding work seeks to promote women's contributions to peacebuilding and civil society dialogue (Spurk 2010, 3–29).

Some CSOs encourage women's input during various phases in the implementation of community projects. Women's CSOs endeavour to make training and campaigning activities as creative as possible to enhance activists' engagement in local peacebuilding actions (Natil 2019). Is women's active participation in local CSOs, social movements, and NGOs a form of local ownership contributing to peacebuilding activities in a conflict zone? Sustainable outcomes are a crucial issue not only for CSOs but also for most international actors engaged in conflict zones (Bojicic-Dzelilovic and Martin 2016).

Some women's CSOs emphasise that their core values of freedom of speech and active participation are as inclusive and broad-based as possible (Natil 2019). Michels and de Graaf (2010) argue that 'citizen participation serves an instrumental rather than an expressive purpose; in practice, participation is not regarded as a value in itself'. This approach considers the experiences of local peacebuilders as agents for peace (Ozerdem and Podder 2015) and how CSOs aim to promote women's effective societal practices in resolving community problems and increasing their power to make social changes in their own communities. This power can be seen through the lenses of empowerment, transformation, and security (Porter 2013), and Pruitt and Lee-Koo (2020) have also studied their leadership in eras of security and peace.

The extent to which CSOs have increased women's contributions to peacebuilding and change processes can be seen through women's power as agents for local peacebuilding, their CSOs' impact on leading a network of local groups, and their cooperation to achieve a real change in terms of peacebuilding, reconciliation, and conflict resolution. Women's local practices in peacebuilding activities have also expanded in a variety of unexpected public and private spaces. Some local CSOs often attempt to create safe local spaces for women by implementing grassroots development and peacebuilding, including post-conflict reconstruction programmes. However, CSOs' efforts to create local spaces for female agents for peacebuilding cannot be achieved without a top-down mechanism as a contribution from the public sector, as Bherer, Dufour, and Montambeault (2016) argue.

The purpose of local networks is to ensure the implementation of effective methodologies to interact with young women activists and to motivate them to share their experiences and civil society success stories with their CSOs (Natil 2016, 2019, 2020a). The activists put their skills into practice through volunteering at CSOs and engaging with their peers to resolve societal problems in their local communities. Local ownership is a significant aspect of peacebuilding and security for CSOs' engagement and delivery at the local or national level, as Hibaaq Osman, founder and CEO of Karam, said when speaking at the launch of IPI's new report on women's participation in Libya on July 26, 2023: 'Localising the WPS agenda and making it relevant to the needs of people on the ground is key to preventing the increasing scrutinisation of WPS!'

This practice makes real improvements to their experiences, knowledge, skills, and public engagement, assisting activists in contributing to their societies (Michels and de Graaf 2010). Young female activists also use digital platforms and local media networks to raise social issues and deliver services to their societies at different times. Local CSOs, such as SVF in Palestine and LWPP in Libya, cooperate and work closely with media networks to produce and broadcast live radio programmes to give young women a platform to express themselves. However, there are still many educated and open-minded people who look at CSOs with suspicion, as Fathi Tomi says: 'But many

Libyans still look at these organisations with suspicious eyes, owing to division, lack of transparency and absence of the state' (Tomi 2017).

This framework presents the lived experiences of grassroots activists/peacebuilders and how they contribute to promoting and increasing young people's participatory contributions to decision-making processes and increasing their power to decide on changes to their own future. This chapter examines the power and impact of the network of local organisations and their coordination and cooperation in undertaking effective actions and campaigns, in order to make change a reality in terms of politics and development. CSOs also encourage participants to share information about their achievements and challenges on social media. Donors demand that partner CSOs share their target group's success stories as part of their public diplomacy activities to show the impact of their activities. LWPP, for instance, has documented its sustainability achievements as follows:

> In the last 9 years, we have reached out to, and built the capacities of more than 100 organizations and individual activists in Libya and in the Diaspora. Our aim is to form and solidify a critical mass of CSOs, activists mobilized to develop, guide, and influence a constructive upwards, and downward dialogue stream towards peacebuilding, whilst ensuring human rights in Libya.
>
> (Libyan Women's Platform for Peace 2023)

Documenting and sharing their stories through well-designed grassroots and international platforms show how they have challenged circumstances to show themselves as agents for peacebuilding in their own communities. A number of Libyan women have made exceptional contributions to their society by defending human rights, democratic processes, and community peacebuilding, both conceptually and in practice, despite the social and political challenges and barriers.

Prospects and Challenges for Local Peacebuilders

Natil (2019, 2020a) has previously discussed the barriers facing CSOs and their activists and their capacities to shift and function within complicated sociocultural, political, and economic contexts. CSOs' activities include helping to eliminate the phenomenon of domestic violence against women. Violence has been a serious challenge to local structure and peacebuilding activists and human rights defenders and will continue to be as long as sustainable peace is non-existent in Libya (Natil 2014, 2019, 2020b).

This represents a serious test of their active engagement in the peacebuilding and human rights development of their societies. Violence is used against women and is a consequence of the unequal power relations within the family specifically and in society in general. The women of Libya and Palestine, for example, have been subject to different types of violence owing to the ongoing conflict, divisions, and the social context. Activists in Libya faced a huge pressure after the assassination of Salwa Bugaighis, a co-founder of LWPP, at her home on June 25, 2014; the assassination of another female parliamentarian, Fariha al-Berkawi, on July 17, 2014; and the disappearance of Siham Sergiwa in Benghazi on July 17, 2019 (Alharathy 2023). Violence and aggression against human rights defenders escalated further after the murder of Hanan al-Barassi by a group of armed men in Benghazi city centre in broad daylight (Human Rights Watch 2020).

Marginalised and vulnerable groups face violence as a major threat to both their civic engagement and community participation. According to Müller and Tranchant (2017), violence against women can take various forms, such as psychological violence, cursing, insults, yelling, and screaming. A UN Women study found in 2017 that 80% of men and 48% of women believe that men should be the decision-makers at home (UN Women & Promundo USA 2017). Women are often described as victims and marginalised from leading formal political and institutional processes, but they are powerful agents for community peacebuilding education in contexts of conflict (Arostegui 2013).

According to Potter (2008), women have long been distinguished at the forefront of peacebuilding efforts. Their engagement in grassroots peacebuilding is much more visible while men take part in formal political processes. Women's integration into all peacebuilding, therefore, is very important in reconstruction and rebuilding processes following periods of conflict (Potter 2008, 142–43). It is necessary to transfer the pulse of grassroots activism to promote reconciliation and to broadcast positive statements rather than incitements and negativity, as well as to ensure the validity of news before its publication in order to refute anything that could disturb community peacebuilding initiatives. Women are still fighting to improve their position and to move from the margins of society to become key decision-makers in civil, political, and community work. Their various missions aim for women's civil rights, public freedoms, and contributions to society—despite living in contexts of conflict. Women's leaders are also still attempting to challenge and change the circumstances and constraints that have already placed women in a worse situation than men (Natil 2019, 2020b).

Sharing information about their challenges and success stories in peacebuilding at various levels in conflict zones is relevant to women's empowerment (Porter 2007). Consequently, an increasing number of young people and women have been fighting against their social and cultural contexts and are willing to claim their rights as a result of awareness-raising and assistance through CSOs.

In addition to the social and political barriers mentioned before, CSOs' human rights defenders and peacebuilding activities also face a number of financial challenges that affect their legitimacy and sustainability (Natil 2020a).

Conclusion

The role of women's CSOs' contribution to local peacebuilding efforts has been an important issue to consider since the failure of the so-called 'Oslo peace process' in Palestine and the failure of the Libyan Revolution. Michels and de Graaf (2010), however, argue that citizen participation is usually considered a significant aspect and has positive effects on the quality of democracy. Young peacebuilders' and human rights defenders' participation can be seen as an outcome of their contribution, power, and influence according to the social, political, and cultural environment of their communities (Natil 2016). This chapter's argument thus runs contrary to the assumption that women acting as CSOs' peacebuilders and human rights defenders in conflict zones have no power to contribute to changes, peace, and development processes in their local communities.

CSOs must be careful to ensure that the implementation of programmes remains inclusive and as broadly based as possible, focusing on empowering women's networks and collective work among civil society actors as a base for sustainable action. Civil society partnerships will ensure the actions' success. They will also ensure their inclusivity and the active civil engagement of activists with participatory approaches. These partnerships' principal methodology involves processes, networks, education, communication, and change (Natil 2019, 2020a).

In addition, local peacebuilders and human rights activists challenged the pandemic despite the major challenges that are a result of the repercussions of the successive crises striking the Palestinian community owing to the ongoing economic, social, political, and funding shifts. These shifts have already imposed a serious challenge to the scope of work and level of intervention of effective CSOs' human rights activists who provide services to the residents of the sector in various fields, such as education, health, improving livelihoods, and unemployment and infrastructure projects. Despite a lack of funding and the periods of lockdown, CSOs' peacebuilders and human rights activists have been working from home and engaging with their communities over the internet. Some CSOs have run awareness activities on social media. Peacebuilders and human rights engagement activists have included running online sessions to raise awareness about how to fight violence against women during the pandemic. This illustrated how they played a significant role in helping the local governance to deal with containing the spread of COVID-19. They engaged with hospitals, community health centres, and clinics while living in severe circumstances, including a lack of human security, owing to political shifts and instability, economic issues, violence, occupation, and a dependency on foreign aid.

References

Alharathy, S. 2023. "After Four Years of Disappearance, Fate of MP Sergiwa Remains Unknown." *Libya Observer*. Accessed September 4, 2023. https://libyaobserver.ly/news/after-four-years-disappearance-fate-mp-sergiwa-remains-unknown

Arostegui, J. 2013. "Gender, Conflict, and Peace-building: How Conflict Can Catalyse Positive Change for Women." *Gender & Development* 21 (3): 533–49. https://doi.org/10.1080/13552074.2013.846624

Berents, B., and S. McEvoy-Levy. 2015. "Theorising Youth and Everyday Peace (Building)." *Peacebuilding* 3 (2): 115–25. https://doi.org/10.1080/21647259.2015.1052627

Bherer, L., P. Dufour, and F. Montambeault. 2016. "The Participatory Democracy Turn: An Introduction." *Journal of Civil Society* 12 (3): 225–30. https://doi.org/10.1080/17448689.2016.1216383

Bojicic-Dzelilovic, V., and M. Martin. 2016. *Local Ownership Challenges in Peacebuilding and Conflict Prevention*. London School of Economics and Political Science.

Cho, A., J. Byrne, and Z. Pelter. 2020. *Digital Civic Engagement by Young People*. UNICEF Offices of Global Insight and Policy. Accessed January 5, 2021. https://www.unicef.org/sites/default/files/2020-07/Digital-civic-engagement-by-young-people-2020_4.pdf

Donais, T. 2012. *Peacebuilding and Local Ownership Post-Conflict Consensus-building*. Routledge.

Gerring, J. 2011. "The Case Study: What It Is and What It Does." In *The Oxford Handbook of Political Science*, edited by Robert E. Goodin, 2–38. Oxford Press University.

Human Rights Watch. 2020. "Libya Outspoken Benghazi Lawyer Murdered." Accessed September 4, 2023. https://www.hrw.org/news/2020/11/11/libya-outspoken-benghazi-lawyer-murdered.

Jad, I. 2018. *The Palestinian Women's Activism: Nationalism, Secularism and Islamism*. New York: Syracuse University Press.

Libyan Women's Platform for Peace (LWPP). Accessed September 3, 2023. https://lwpp.org/projects/details/19/LWPP_Highlights_the_Role_of_Women_in_Mediation_and_Reconciliation_in_Libya

McEvoy-Levy, S. 2006. *Troublemakers or Peacemakers: Youth and Post-Accord Peacebuilding*. University of Notre Dame Press.

Merrill, R. C. 2017. "The Middle Eastern Gender Gap: The State of Female Political Participation Before, During and After the 'Arab Spring'." In *The Arab Spring, Civil Society, and Innovative Activism,* edited by C. Çakmak, 121–40. London: Palgrave Macmillan Publishers Ltd.

Michels, A., and L. De Graaf. 2010. "Examining Citizen Participation: Local Participatory Policy Making and Democracy." *Local Government Studies* 36 (4): 477–91. https://doi.org/10.1080/03003930.2010.494101

Müller, C., and J. Tranchant. 2017. "International Institute for Environment and Development." Accessed June 4, 2020. https://www.jstor.org/stable/resrep02733.

Natil, I. 2014. "A Shifting Political Landscape: NGOs' Civic Activism and Response in the Gaza Strip, 1967–2014." *Journal of Peacebuilding & Development* 9 (3): 82–87. https://doi.org/10.1080/15423166.2014.983369

Natil, I. 2016. "The Challenges and Opportunities of Donor-driven Aid to Youth Refugees in Palestine." *Journal of Peacebuilding & Development* 11 (2): 78–82. http://dx.doi.org/10.1080/15423166.2016.1197791

Natil, I. 2019. "The Power of Civil Society: Young Leaders' Engagement in Non-violent Actions in Palestine." In *The Power of Civil Society in the Middle East and North Africa: Peacebuilding, Change and Development*, edited by I. Natil, C. Pieroban, and L. Tauber 24–36. New York: Routledge.

Natil, I. 2020a. "Introducing Barriers to Effective Civil Society Organisations." In *Barriers to Effective Civil Society Organisations: Political, Social and Financial Shifts*, edited by I. Natil, V. Malila, and Y. Sai, 9–17. New York: Routledge.

Natil, I. 2020b. "Women's Community Peacebuilding in the Occupied Palestinian Territories (OPT)." In *The Palgrave Encyclopedia of Peace and Conflict Studies*, edited by O. Richmond and G. Visoka, 1–12. Cham: Palgrave Macmillan. https://doi.org/10.1007/978-3-030-11795-5_47-1

Noma, E., D. Aker, and J. Freeman. 2012. "Heeding Women's Voices: Breaking Cycles of Conflict and Deepening the Concept of Peacebuilding." *Journal of Peacebuilding & Development* 7 (1): 7–32. https://doi.org/10.1080/15423166.2012.719384

Ozerdem, A., and S. Podder. 2015. *Youth in Conflict and Peacebuilding*. Palgrave.

Paffenholz, T. 2010. *Civil Society & Peacebuilding: A Critical Assessment*. Boulder, CO: Lynne Rienner.

Paffenholz, T., and C. Spurk. 2010. "A Comprehensive Analytical Framework." In *Civil Society & Peacebuilding: A Critical Assessment*, edited by T. Paffenholz, 65–75. Boulder, CO: Lynne Rienner.

Peters, K., and S. El Taraboulsi-McCarthy. 2020. "Opinion: Dealing with COVID-19 in Conflict Zones Needs a Different Approach." *Thomson Reuters Foundation*, Accessed July 24, 2020. https://news.trust.org/item/20200329200250-bj72i/

Porter, E. 2007. *Peacebuilding: Women in International Perspective*. London: Routledge.

Porter, E. 2013. "Rethinking Women's Empowerment." *Journal of Peacebuilding & Development* 8 (1): 1–14. https://doi.org/10.1080/15423166.2013.785657

Potter, M. 2008. *Women, Civil Society and Peacebuilding in Northern Ireland: Paths to Peace through Women's Empowerment*. Taylor & Francis.

Pruitt, L., and K. Lee-Koo. 2020. *Young Women and Leadership*. Routledge.

Spurk, C. 2010. "Understanding Civil Society." In *Civil Society & Peacebuilding: A Critical Assessment,* edited by T. Paffenholz, 3–26. Boulder, CO: Lynne Rienner.

Tomi, F. 2017. "A Libyan Activist". Interviewed. Accessed September 25, 2017.

UNICEF. 2020b. "Youth Led Initiative Fund Launched on International Volunteering Day. A New Youth Led Initiative Fund to support volunteering." *Press Release*. Accessed January 4, 2021. https://www.unicef.org/jordan/press-releases/youth-led-initiative-fund-launched-international-volunteering-day

UN Women & Promundo USA. 2017. "Understanding Masculinities: International Men and Gender Equality Survey (IMAGES) – Middle East and North Africa, Egypt, Lebanon, Morocco, and Palestine." Accessed June 9, 2020. https://promundoglobal.org/wp-content/uploads/2017/05/IMAGES-MENA-Multi-Country-Report-EN-16May2017-web.pdf.

7 Foreign Aid

Challenges to Local Economy of Civil Society of Jordan

Ghazi Al-Assaf

Introduction

Civil society organizations (CSOs) in Jordan have had foreign aid as not only a vital resource but also, at the same time, a source of concern. A high dependency on foreign sources has been questioned for the credibility and viability of indigenous CSOs. Usually, CSOs face challenges in reconciling donor agendas with community goals, fulfilling reporting expectations, and preserving their independence in this financing environment. Foreign donors' conditions and priorities have at times shaped the activities of local CSOs in a way that is out of sync with the grassroots' needs. This has led to the competitive funding environment that has negatively impacted on the coordination between the CSOs and may at the same time alter the priorities of the Jordanian civil society. However, the local ownership for CSOs entails identifying ways of creating self-reliance and less dependence on foreign funding, possibly through local giving, social businesses, or government support. This financial independence is very important to ensure the effectiveness of CSOs to be the true voice of the civil society in Jordan.

Foreign aid has been used in the international relations system to enhance the development of the recipient countries in terms of their economic as well as social status. However, the relations between foreign aid and the local economy are not always as straightforward as desired and may present various problems that are not easy to anticipate, especially in countries that have rather specific sociopolitical systems. In this chapter, we consider the challenges the Hashemite Kingdom of Jordan, a country that has been receiving foreign aid for long, faced in its civil society and the economy due to foreign aid. As it is situated in the core of the Middle East, Jordan has been subjected to various economic and social problems in its history. Its strategic location on top of being a relatively stable country in a very unstable region has made it to be a top target country for foreign assistance by a wide group of international donors and organizations.

Examining the effects of foreign aid on the Jordanian economy is one of the main concerns of this chapter. The current chapter will also discuss how

DOI: 10.4324/9781003565048-7

outside sources of resources can change the market conditions by impacting the market conditions of domestic industries and business. The subject of aid dependency and its effects on the economic risks and the problems faced by harmonizing the objectives of foreign aid with the local economic situation will be discussed in this chapter. Moreover, we will examine the way foreign aid shapes the making of economic policies in Jordan, which can perhaps transform Jordan into a country that implements policies that do not necessarily align to its paths of long-term economic growth.

Moreover, the chapter will present an evaluation of the effect of foreign aid on the civil society of Jordan. Civil society organizations should be able to effect change, advocate for the rights of the oppressed, and check on power. This chapter will build on the ways in which foreign aid can define the civil society in Jordan and the subsequent strategies of domestic organizations. We will also look at the difficulties of how to effectively utilize the foreign aid and not undermine the sovereignty and the relation with the grassroots base of the civil society organizations. This chapter will also look at how, while foreign aid is intended to help, it can have a negative impact on civil society in the aid-receiving country by creating parallel structures of support or by diverting resources and individuals away from local endeavors. Additionally, the Syrian crisis changed the character of economy, society, and how the foreign aid operates within the host country of Jordan. This chapter explores the spillovers of such a paradigm shift on Jordan's civil society organizations (CSOs) and their shifting functions during the refugee crisis.

This chapter aims at generating questions on the possibility of improving the strategies through which economic aid is provided to countries like Jordan in the future. This means that by criticizing the current strategies of aid, it is possible to contribute to a discussion on how aid can be made more effective and, crucially, how it can be made less foreign. This analysis is especially relevant today at a time when the place and effect of foreign aid are under global consideration, and there is a search for the most optimal ways of assisting the developing nations. It also aims at revealing the effects of foreign aid in Jordan by analyzing the relationship between external assistance and internal factors. This analysis gives not only the relevant information about the particular case of Jordan but also an opportunity to look at the similar problems in other countries that receive aid. In this regard, the aim of this chapter is to provide a more detailed analysis of the ways in which foreign aid can be more effectively targeted toward the particular priorities and capabilities of the recipient countries and communities.

The Main Trend in Foreign Aid Flows to Jordan

Many countries include foreign aid in their development program and plan, and Jordan is one of these countries. Jordan has faced numerous economic challenges, regional crises in the region, and shortages of resources and thus has relied on the international community for funding of its development strategies and economic stability. Foreign aid to developing countries like Jordan serves multiple purposes: it assists in plugging gaps in national budgets, supports major capital investments, boosts social spending, and assists in managing shocks and population movements such as refugees.

According to the Jordan's Ministry of Planning and International Cooperation Foreign Assistance Report (2023), which shows all the types of aid received by Jordan from other countries, the foreign assistance is divided into three main categories: Grants, Soft Loans, and Technical Assistance as well as Capacity Building measures. Grants is the category of financial aid, and there are several subcategories. It includes the Budget Support or Sector Budget Support which in its essence refers to the provision of funds to the government of Jordan in its general budget or in specific sectors. The other subcategory is Support for Development Priorities/Projects which import positive funding for some development goals and objectives of Jordan. It also contains the additional Grants to support Jordan Response Plan to the Syrian Crisis. This also has implications for the role of regional geopolitical events such as the Syrian crisis in the aid diplomacy of Jordan. The report also sustains this with the Budget Support, Host Communities, and Refugee/Humanitarian funding as the main areas of this crisis response.

The second major category of the instrument is Soft Loans, which entails offering cash to Jordan at a low-cost rate of interest than what is prevailing in the market for commercial loans and at a more extended time to adjust the loan. Under this category, there are two subcategories: Development Projects and Budget Support or Sector Budget Support. This means that Soft Loans are used not only for specific projects but also for the general support of the budget which makes Jordan a not fully reckless borrower but more convenient in financial terms.

The third type of foreign assistance to Jordan is Technical Assistance and Capacity Building, which deals with the non-tangible support. This category is further grouped into two—the institutional and the human Capacity Building. The latter is further subdivided into Training Programs and Scholarships which show the part that Jordan plays in building the capacity of its population. In addition, the previous category has subcategories of Experts, Volunteers, Feasibility Studies, and Twinning Programs.

Such an approach to classify foreign assistance reveals that the assistance to Jordan is diversified and not very clear cut. It reveals that the aid is not just a money transfer sent to the country but also a range of measures that can be categorized as tactical and strategic and are directed toward the development goals. The provision of the crisis-related support also gives the idea about the way that foreign aid is sensitive to the changes in the dynamics of the region and the new humanitarian challenges which appear there.

In addition, the Jordan's Ministry of Planning and International Cooperation Foreign Assistance Report shows the distribution of foreign aid to Jordan by sector for the year 2023. It can be easily understood from this report how the international aid is being spent in various sectors of the economy and the society of Jordan. The single most apparent fact captured in the report is that budget support takes the lead with more than 41% of the total foreign aid to Jordan. This considerable allocation implies that a major share of aid is targeted at financing Jordan's fiscal stability and government functions. This is due to the fact that extensive budget support shows that the international community appreciates the macroeconomic problems of Jordan and the necessity to strengthen the country's fiscal base.

Water and sanitation are the second on the list of sectors that attract foreign aid with 14.4% of the total. This enormous funding is evidence of the importance of water in Jordan, a country that is among those having the most water scarcity in the world. The allocation indicates that more focus has been directed on enhancing water supply and treatment systems and water and sanitation services' delivery to the population.

The third highest sector that benefits from the foreign aid is food security and agriculture with the share of 13.2%. This large allocation underlines the need to address the food security and to support the agricultural sector in Jordan which is a water-deficient and arid country. The attention to this sector most probably is meant to increase self-sufficiency in food production in Jordan and reduce the effects of the volatility in the surrounding region on food security. Social protection receives 11.7% of the foreign assistance; this reflects the government of Jordan's commitment to ensure that the needy and the most vulnerable groups of the society are protected, and there is a strong safety net to support them. This sector may include a number of projects that are targeted at combating poverty, supporting refugees and other vulnerable groups of population.

Economic development and employment, vocational training, and education and livelihood are dominating on about 4% each, which indicates the commitment of the country in enhancing the education sector in Jordan as a vital element of development and human capital. Other sectors receive smaller but still significant portions of the aid: These include Economic Diversification and Infrastructure Development (1.6%), Human Development—Health (1%), Natural Resource Management—Environment (1.2%), and Governance and Accountability—Good Governance and Justice (2.3%). These allocations show that there is an all-round plan for development that covers several aspects of the society and the economy. However, there are other sectors that obtain very little share of aid, including Tourism with 0.36%, Energy with 0.1%, Youth and Culture with 0.1%, and Information and Communications Technology with 0.1% (Foreign Assistance Report 2023, 16).

The Major Donors and Shifting Aid Priorities in Jordan

The picture of foreign aid to Jordan for the last decade is a complex one, given the fact that many different countries and organizations have been involved with their own agendas. The current section of this chapter delves on the main actors in assisting Jordan and shift in their concentration in the country's growth and stability.

The European Union and the member states of this union are also among the major supporters of the organization. The EU provided Jordan with €765 million of bilateral assistance for the period of 2014–2020 under the European Neighbourhood Instrument (European Commission 2021). This aid has aimed at the support of the rule of law, employment generation, and the private sector development. Germany, for instance, has been quite active with a contribution of €483 million in 2021, much of which has gone into water sector development and refugee assistance (German Federal Ministry for Economic Cooperation and Development 2022).

The Gulf Cooperation Council (GCC) states have also provided lots of support to Jordan in this regard. In 2018, the three GCC countries of Saudi Arabia, the UAE, and Kuwait committed to provide $2.5 billion. Applicants also include Jordan which received a $5 billion aid package to support its economy (Reuters 2018). This support was in the form of budget support, development aid, and guarantees to the World Bank for the support of Jordan. Nevertheless, the real distribution and application of GCC aid have been a function of political and economic cycles in the region. Japan has always been an active player in the development of Jordan. JICA data shows that Japan's aid to Jordan in the period between 2011 and 2020 was about $1.3 billion, which is mainly aimed at water resource management, energy, and assistance to Syrian refugees (JICA 2021).

International financial institutions have been involved in the restructuring of the Jordanian economy and its enhancement. The current active portfolio of the World Bank Group in Jordan consists of 12 projects with total commitments of $2 billion. These projects are in various sectors including education, energy, and social protection. The International Monetary Fund (IMF) has also been of great assistance, giving out about $1 billion to support Jordan's economic and financial reform program (IMF 2020). The Syrian refugee crisis has been the most influential crisis on the donor's priorities in the last ten years. The Jordan Response Plan (JRP) for the Syria Crisis 2020–2022 was targeting to raise a total of $6 billion. This was required for the Syrian refugees and the host communities needs in Jordan (Jordan Response Platform for the Syria Crisis 2020). This has led to increased discharge of humanitarian assistance and development aid where Germany for example has provided a large sum of money toward the support of refugees.

The issue of climate change and environmental concerns have of late gained much attention from the development partners. For instance the Green

Growth National Action Plan 2021–2025 has been sponsored by different donors including the EU that has promised €39 million for green growth and circular economy projects in Jordan (Ministry of Environment, Jordan 2020). Since 2020, the COVID-19 pandemic also shifted the focus of donors in a new direction. For instance, the World Bank provided $20 million in the year 2020 to support Jordan in dealing with the current health crisis and to increase its ability to face it (World Bank 2020). Similarly, the EU offered more than €200 million in the year 2020 to support Jordan in fighting the pandemic (European Commission 2020).

Looking through the trends of the foreign aid in Jordan in the last decade, one can see geopolitical fights, development strategies, and responses to new challenges. Moreover, over time, attention has moved toward what we could say are the most important topics that today appear as classical dyadic approaches—that is, assistance to refugees, climate change, and pandemic diseases. Detours in the donor geography, in terms of refugee aid and foreign assistance, constitute an eloquent testimony of the fragility of foreign assistance and its importance in the future of the country.

The Economic Impact of Foreign Aid to Jordan

The economy of Jordan has developed entirely because of foreign aid, which in one way or the other has controlled its growth as well as the market. This chapter aims to investigate the relationship between foreign assistance and Jordan's economy by looking into the dependency on assistance and the influence of assistance on the local economy. For a long time, Jordan's economic development has relied heavily on foreign aid. The World Bank reports that net official development assistance to Jordan amounted to more than $3 billion in 2021. In 2021, the country committed to spending 8% of its Gross National Income (GNI), a level which has been sustained for the past ten years (World Bank 2021). Jordan is on the list of the most aided in the Middle East because it is highly dependent on aid. Even more important is this aid when trying to analyze Jordan's budget. For instance in the year 2019, due to 100% of the total funding foreign Grants could not reach an extent of more than 13%. The Ministry of Finance, Jordan 2020 reports that it accounts for 3% of country total budget revenue. This has been very important, especially when it comes to dealing with regional crises and economic shocks of the recent past of the region.

The effect of foreign aid on Jordan's economy is complex and sometimes even contradictory. In one hand, aid has played a crucial role in supporting infrastructure, social services, and economic adjustment. For instance USAID has provided more than $1 billion since 1950s, and America through USAID has spent over $6 billion in an effort to solve the water scarcity challenges that limit economic development worldwide (USAID 2022). It is in this context that such investments in the social infrastructure can be seen to have helped in laying the foundation for the growth of the economy (Al-Ahmad 1992). However, the flow of foreign aid has also had some negative impact on local markets and industries. In this regard, we can consider the most well-known effect that is the so-called "Dutch Disease", where large inflows of foreign currency—in this case through aid—can cause the local currency to strengthen, which hurts export industries and helps import industries. As to the extent of this effect in Jordan, it is rather challenging to provide a specific number; however, the literature has pointed out that aid inflows have led to an appreciation of real exchange rate which may negatively affect the development of export-oriented industries (Karras 2006).

This has also been coupled with the provision of aid which in one way or the other has given rise to aid dependency which may not be very friendly to local business and enterprise. As at the time of writing this chapter, the Jordan Enterprise Development Corporation (JEDCO) had estimated that the SMEs accounted for about 98% of the total enterprises in Jordan, but their contribution to the GDP was still very low at about 30% (JEDCO 2019). This, therefore, implies that even with the many resources that have been pumped into the private sector with the aim of promoting the local industries, they may not be as efficient as expected.

Another effect is also on the local labour markets, which is also significant in the current analysis. While employment might be created during the implementation of foreign aid projects, the same can lead to wage disparity between the workers in aid-funded projects and the prevailing market wage. As cited by the Jordan Strategy Forum, the salaries in the international organizations and the foreign-funded projects are between 200 and 300% higher than those of the local private sector for similar positions (Jordan Strategy Forum 2018). Thus, this inequality may lead to the migration of human capital from other local industries into the aided projects, which may be prejudicial to the development of the private sector.

On the other hand, there is evidence that foreign aid has been very helpful in helping Jordan to cope with what would have been devastating shocks to its economy. For instance the Syrian refugees who came into Jordan since 2011 have caused a strain on the economy of Jordan. Published literature such as the Jordan Compact which aimed at turning the refugee crisis into a development one has been instrumental. Approximatively one US dollar has been mobilized via the Jordan Compact. The United States has offered $6 billion in Grants and concessional loans; it has provided support toward employment opportunities for the locals and the Syrian refugees (Center for Global Development 2020).

This was also enhanced by the COVID-19 pandemic which exposed the fact that Jordan remains an economy that cannot sustain itself without the support of donor aid. The international donors provided a fairly substantial assistance to Jordan during the crisis. The IMF has endorsed $1 billion.

Jordan obtained $2 billion from the Extended Fund Facility in March 2020 and $396 million in emergency assistance in May 2020 (IMF 2020). It was crucial for Jordan to obtain this external support to mitigate the effects of the pandemic on the economy in a rather short time.

Challenges of CSOs and Foreign Aid

The relationship between foreign aid and CSOs in Jordan is not usually straightforward, but it is crucial to analyze potential and challenges. This chapter is an attempt to identify and analyze how foreign aid modifies the work, the decision-making, and the environment of CSOs in Jordan, demonstrating the complexity of these relations. However, one of the most important problems with foreign aid provided to Jordan's CSOs is that of sustainability and future perspectives. Many organizations have become highly dependent on external sources of finance that are both volatile and unreliable and which rely on donors' changing agendas. According to a survey conducted by the Konrad-Adenauer-Stiftung, more than 80% of Jordanian CSOs obtain their funding from foreign donors (KAS 2019). For that reason, these organizations are vulnerable, in the sense that they exist by the goodwill and funding of international donors and as such cannot provide coherent and durable programs and maintain staff.

The policies and goals of the foreign donors affect the actions of the local CSOs in a way that sometimes the donor's agendas do not match the needs of the local communities. In the same way, many CSOs discover that they have to design their programs based on the donor requirements instead of the needs of the people on the ground. For example, after the Syrian refugee crisis, there was a clear change in the focus of the funding toward the programs that are related to refugees. Although this was a vital task, it made many CSOs to shift their attention and concentrate on this agenda at the expense of other key local concerns. The Al-Hayat Center for Civil Society Development highlighted that between 2011 and 2018, more than half of the new CSO projects in northern Jordan were refugee focused, and this could be attributed to the fact that funders had shifted their focus to such projects (Al-Hayat Center 2019).

Still, there is the problem of paperwork associated with the foreign aid implementation. Many a times, CSOs face challenges in reporting procedures, financial management, and assessment and evaluation requirements set by international donors. According to a research carried out by the USAID Civil Society Program in Jordan, small- and medium-sized CSOs indicated that they use 30% of their employees' time in performing donor compliance and reporting (USAID Civil Society Program 2020). These kinds of overhead can slow down the actual projects and hinder the organizations from being very responsive to the needs of the local communities (Sander 2023).

The existence of foreign aids has also influenced collaboration and coordination of CSOs in Jordan in many ways. In the same way, some donor-driven interventions have promoted partnership and coalition formation among organizations. For instance the EU-funded "Support to Civil Society in Jordan" program that was initiated in the year 2018 has as one of its goals the enhancement of linkages and formation of coalitions between CSOs (European Union External Action 2018). But the competition for funds has also been a source of rivalry and duplication of effort among the CSOs. This means that the organizations are at times in a competition for the same source of funding which may hamper collaboration and sharing of information.

The effect of foreign aid on CSO agendas has created concerns on the ownership of the civil society agenda. The problem is that this dependence on foreign funding may actually be skewing the priorities of the Jordanian civil society. According to the Carnegie Endowment for International Peace, many of the Jordanian CSOs were more focused on the latest jargon in use in the international development discourse than the needs of the people on the ground. The legal and regulatory framework for CSOs in Jordan has also been influenced by the logic of foreign aid. The government has had an enabling and a restrictive policy toward the funding of CSOs from foreign sources at different times. For example, the 2008 Law on Societies put a ban on foreign funding of CSOs until this was slightly eased in 2009, and then the ban was reinstated in 2017 with more stringent measures (International Center for Not-for-Profit Law 2021). These policy shifts have been occasioned by geopolitical factors and the perception of foreign interference, which makes the environment in which CSOs depending on foreign funding operate unstable.

The effects of foreign aid on the professionalization of the CSOs in Jordan is another factor that should be looked at. Because of the donor requirements, there has been an enhanced organizational development in areas like financial management and project planning, but there is the fear of the emergence of what has been termed as an NGO elite. This is a phenomenon where a small number of organizations, which are well funded and professionally managed, take over the sector and create a rift between it and the grassroots movements as well as small organizations. According to the Jordan Civil Society Index, the share of the top 10% of the CSOs in Jordan of the total foreign funding allocation to the sector was over 70% in 2020 (CIVICUS 2020).

The COVID-19 pandemic has only served to bring both the importance of foreign aid and the problems of CSOs in Jordan into sharper focus. Community assistance during the crisis was provided by numerous organizations that sometimes received funds from international donors. But the pandemic also highlights the challenges of aid-dependent CSOs because some of the donors have diverted the funds or even stopped supporting certain programs, leaving CSOs in a quandary. As many as 40% of the surveyed civil society organizations (CSOs) in Jordan had to pause some or all of their operations because of the funding constraints stemming from the COVID-19 crisis, according to a snapshot evaluation by the UN Development Program in 2020.

Best Strategies in Maintaining Effective CSOs' Work in Jordan

Another emerging issue that CSOs, in the context of Jordan, desperately solved in today's world is how to address all the issues connected with the aid while staying independent and effective. This discussion aims at categorizing the aforementioned challenges and mapping how CSOs can effectively endeavor to overcome them by referring to the existing literature and real-case studies from the Jordanian context. CSOs have employed one of the major approaches for organizational independence—that is, the use of multiple sources of funding. Organizations which depend largely on funding from a single donor or a few donors can easily be influenced, plus funding sources can easily be withdrawn. The West Asia-North Africa (WANA) Institute previously published their research examining the link between the fund sources of Jordanian CSOs and their programmatic cohesion and propensity to surrender to governments' demands on altering their mandate; according to the research, Jordanian CSOs with diverse funds were more programmatic and consistent (WANA Institute 2019). For example, the Jordan River Foundation, one of the most effective Jordanian NGO, has realized to search for the additional sources of funding from the international donors, Jordanian companies, and income-generating activities. The current approach has enabled the organization to prioritize child safety and community participation though adapting to change of donor interests and emphasize (Jordan River Foundation Annual Report 2020).

In addition, maintaining autonomy, the approach focuses on the development of local funding sources. The culture of local philanthropy is still not as rich in Jordan as, for example, in Anglo-Saxon countries, but it is possible to build it further. A good and inspiring example can be seen in the experience of Ruwwad Al-Tanmeya organization. Ruwwad was established by some young and pioneering local businessmen and has evolved a grant-making approach in which funds from corporate social responsibility programs and other private and public sources are managed for people-initiated and -controlled community-based development. From related sources of fund of the Ruwwad for the year 2020, it has been observed that funding source from the local sponsors exceeded more than 60% hence creating and maintaining of strong social connection and community relations (Ruwwad Annual Report 2020).

CSOs can continue functioning and remain independent by building better governance systems and organizational capabilities. When the organizations have strong boards composed of directors drawn from the local communities, they stand a better chance in protecting themselves from being influenced by extraneous forces and keeping the core objectives of the organizations in perspective. It can be illustrated by the example of the Information and Research Center—King Hussein Foundation (IRCKHF). The organization has had a diverse locally based board that has enabled it to adapt well to changing donor environment as well as its research to ensure that it puts out evidence-based policy information (IRCKHF Governance Report 2019).

CSOs can also benefit from collaboration and coalitions in their relations with donors and to avoid dependence on them. In 2018, over 100 Jordanian organizations have come together to form the Jordan NGOs Forum aimed as a response to face simultaneously development issues and development partners and government. The smaller civil society organizations, this has allowed them to participate in formulating the donor agenda and withstand pressure from the individual donors. The values of these issues are very important for donors in the eyes of CSOs, not to mention in the eyes of the target population. CSOs can show funders that they are effective and efficient in the use of resources by proving that they are effective and efficient in their use of resources and, in the process, can have more favorable funding arrangements. Most active in this respect has been the Arab Renaissance for Democracy and Development (ARDD), which has filed clear financial reports and surveys of the results of the organization. This has enabled ARDD to foster long-term relations with the donors and take its time to focus on human rights and access to justice (ARDD Transparency Report 2020).

Other strategies to be employed by the CSOs to improve their effectiveness and capacity-catching service delivery are Capacity Building and knowledge transfer. It could reduce the use of external consultants that are often employed in donor projects. The staff of the Phenix Center for Economic and Informatics Studies have also benefited from successful internal training in research methods and policy analysis. The organization has been able to generate quality research, relevant to the context of the country and reasonably without relying heavily on outside consultants (Phenix Center Annual Report 2020).

The policy dialogue and CSO-operating environment area is another big area of focus. In this manner, CSOs can participate in the development strategies' definition and aid modalities to enhance the environment for their actions. There have been most initiatives undertaken by the Al-Hayat Center for Civil Society Development, and it has been releasing policy briefs on civil society in Jordan and advocating with the government and the donors (2019-2021).

Finally, CSOs can only remain so effective if they have a strong bond with the communities that they work with. Donors' priorities may be changing, and continuous dialogue with the target population and engaging the stakeholders at the planning and implementation of the CSO programs will help in this regard. Some of the Jordanian CSOs use the Community Development Committee (CDC) model, which is more illustrative. These are community-level structures that make the program community-led thus, they have a proper ownership (UNDP Jordan, Community Resilience Case Study 2020).

Conclusion

The paradoxical relationship between the foreign aid, the Jordanian economy, and the work of civil society organizations is a picture of the possibilities and risks. The intent of this chapter has been to map out these different interconnections to derive different conclusions, which form the basis for understanding how aid has been involved in Jordan's development progression. First, it should be noted that Jordan is one of the most aid-dependent countries in the region and that aid continues to make up part of the country's Gross National Income and continues to be an important source of budget support. While this aid has meant so much for the development of Jordan, water in specific, and refugees, it has also brought a dependency which is a little disconcerting from the perspective of sustainability.

Jordan's income and role in its development, including water supply and facilities, and the handling of refugees, has been greatly enhanced by foreign aid. The reliance on this, though, is a worry for the future and economic independence. Foreign aid has turned out to be a double-edged sword in the Jordanian local economy. But, in another way, it has advanced the infrastructure development, social development, and liberalization of the economy. However, what is being funded by aid is also being blamed for some negative effects like possible causing what can be termed as the "Dutch Disease", wage in equality between jobs funded by aid and other market jobs, and suppression of enterprise and private business.

Foreign aid for civil society organizations (CSOs) in Jordan has been both beneficial and with several concerns. The use of foreign funds has also cast a doubt on the autonomy of the local NGOs as the sole representatives of the civil society. One of the problems that these organizations encounter include the pressure to meet the expectations of the donors while at the same time trying to meet the needs of the societies they operate in.

The priorities which the foreign donors have embraced have influenced the operations of the local CSOs in such a way that there is little emphasis on the local issues that deserve attention. This has created a situation where funding is relatively competitive, and there are probably negative implications for coordination between the CSOs and it may also tilt the priorities of the civil society in Jordan.

However, even with regard to the effects of foreign aid and the development which occurred as a result of it, one can raise doubts concerning the stability of the development in the long term. While help saved Jordan from a lot of risk such as Syrian refugees and COVID-19, it seems to have demotivated resource mobilization at home and efficient utilization. The problem that Jordan meets turns into the question of transition from the model of aid receptiveness to the model of aid appropriateness in which foreign aid would initiate the development that might be sustainable in the local context. In the long run, the sustainability of the aid-dependent model of development has to be put into question. Although aid has been one of the solutions that helped Jordan overcome many crises, it may have worked against the country's domestic resource mobilization and efficient allocation.

Regarding the CSOs, another question is whether they are able to remain independent and effective in the light of problems associated with foreign aid. This entails the diversification of the resources and funding, development of the local funding source, enhancement of the governance and institutional frameworks for CSOs, augmentation of the cooperation among CSOs, enhancement of the accountability measures, and the sustainment of the core mandates to the local communities.

In other words, there is a fork when it comes to the foreign aid and the local economy in Jordan and definitely the civil society. Donor support remains a popular theme in the Jordanian narrative, but the state of affairs in the current sociology is how to leverage this kind of help and emerging forms of foreign aid for bottom-up development. This will require yet a further policy action by institutions and step-by-step replacement of the unequal power relationship and cooperation between Jordan and the CSOs with the IDAs.

The challenge of development, as Jordan continues its steady march forward, will be how to fine—how to build upon foreign aid, while creating and strengthening the structures that will codify growth as a locally owned endeavor. This balanced approach will be crucial in ensuring that FAD is utilized to foster the idea of sustainable development—not for grooming the recipients into becoming submissive third-world economies and civil societies that lack true representation and that are rather controlled by the figures abroad.

The chapter provides several recommendations to these challenges such as diversifying the sources of funding, enhancing the local ownership in the development processes, improving the coordination of the donors, creating a conducive environment for CSOs, increasing the accountability in the use of aid, building the capacity of CSOs and other stakeholders, and encouraging economic diversification. Thus, Jordan is confronted with the main task of using foreign aid to foster the culture of independence and home-grown development. This demands strategic policy development; organizational change; and a phased shift in the relations between Jordan, civil society, and the international development partners. The problem therefore lies in how to capture the best of foreign aid without compromising the country's efforts toward self-reliance, sustainable development.

References

Al-Ahmad, A. K. 1992. *Economic Effects of Foreign Aid: Case of Jordan*. University of Missouri-Columbia.

Al-Hayat Center for Civil Society Development. 2019. "Shifts in Civil Society Focus: Analysis of Project Themes 2011–2018, Amman, Jordan."

Al-Hayat Center for Civil Society Development. 2019–2021. "Policy Brief Series on Civil Society Space in Jordan." (Policy Briefs), Amman, Jordan.

Arab Renaissance for Democracy and Development (ARDD). 2020. Al Nahda Amid COVID-19, ARDD's Annual Report 2020.

Center for Global Development. 2020. "The Jordan Compact: Lessons Learnt and Implications for Future Refugee Compacts." (Policy Paper).

CIVICUS. 2020. *Jordan Civil Society Index*. UNDP Report.

European Commission. 2020. "EU Response to Coronavirus in Jordan." *Press Release*.

European Commission. 2021. "European Neighborhood Policy and Enlargement Negotiations: Jordan." https://neighbourhood-enlargement.ec.europa.eu/european-neighbourhood-policy/southern-neighbourhood_en

European Union External Action. 2018. "Support to Civil Society in Jordan." (Program Document).

German Federal Ministry for Economic Cooperation and Development. 2022. "Cooperation with Jordan." https://www.giz.de/en/worldwide/360.html

Information and Research Center – King Hussein Foundation (IRCKHF). 2019. "Governance Report." (Annual Report).

International Center for Not-for-Profit Law. 2021. "Civic Freedom Monitor: Jordan." https://www.icnl.org/resources/civic-freedom-monitor/jordan

International Monetary Fund (IMF). 2020. "IMF Executive Board Approves US$1.3 Billion Extended Arrangement under the Extended Fund Facility for Jordan." (Press Release).

Japan International Cooperation Agency (JICA). 2021. "JICA's Cooperation in Jordan." https://www.jica.go.jp/Resource/jordan/english/activities/activity02.html

Jordan Enterprise Development Corporation (JEDCO). 2019. *SME Sector Analysis*. Report.

Jordan Response Platform for the Syria Crisis. 2020. "Jordan Response Plan for the Syria Crisis 2020–2022." (Policy Document).

Jordan River Foundation. 2020. "Annual Report."

Jordan Strategy Forum. 2018. "Salary Disparities between Local and International Organizations in Jordan." (Research Paper).

Karras, G. 2006. "Foreign Aid and Long-run Economic Growth: Empirical Evidence for a Panel of Developing Countries." *Journal of International Development (The Journal of the Development Studies Association)* 18 (1): 15–28.

Konrad-Adenauer-Stiftung (KAS). 2019. "Civil Society in Jordan: A Literature Review." (Research Paper).

Ministry of Environment, Jordan. 2020. "Green Growth National Action Plan 2021–2025." (Policy Document).

Ministry of Finance, Jordan. 2020. "General Budget Report. Amman, Jordan."

Ministry of Planning and International Cooperation, Foreign Assistance Report. 2023. "Amman, Jordan."
Phenix Center for Economic and Informatics Studies. 2020. "Annual Report."
Reuters. 2018. "Gulf States Pledge $2.5 Billion Aid Package to Jordan." (News Article).
Ruwwad Al-Tanmeya. 2020. "Annual Report."
Sander, A. 2023. "Rethinking Shrinking Civic Space in the Global Souths–How Development Donors Contribute to the Restriction of Civil Society in Jordan." *Democratization* 30 (1): 22–39.
UNDP Jordan. 2020. "Community Resilience Case Study." (Report).
USAID Civil Society Program. 2020. "Survey on CSO Administrative Burdens." (Research Report).
WANA Institute. 2019. "Funding Diversification among Jordanian CSOs: Impacts and Challenges." (Research Paper).
World Bank. 2020. "World Bank Support to Jordan's COVID-19 Pandemic Response."
World Bank. 2021. "World Development Indicators – Jordan."

8 New Implications and Directions for Local Ownership Responses

Ibrahim Natil

This book distinguishes itself as a new approach to civil society in the global south context by focusing on local ownership and the different perspectives for each country, leadership culture, and development in practice. The book reflects on CSOs in development, politics, and business and their impact on community development initiatives and local change processes in these selected countries. The debate and argument are supported by some fieldwork, participatory observation, interviews, and references to the existing literature. This new approach is particularly strong because it is based not only on empirical discussions of individual countries but also on a firm theoretical framework of the discussion of CSO's local ownership, leadership, and development issues. In this way, our book significantly contributes to theoretical discussions of the complexities of civil society organisations' responses to conflict and wars of CSOs in Sub-Saharan Africa, Libya, Yemen, Lebanon, Palestine, and Syria.

High levels of uncertainty as a result of conflict and militarism have presented significant challenges for these societies. These societies in the global south region are resilient and defiant when coping with shifts and changes. By assessing individual contexts and engaging policymakers with rigorous empirical research in a systematic way, CSOs can work to overcome both the internal and external challenges they have faced during the crisis such as wars, conflicts, and diseases. The book is addressed to undergraduates, postgraduates, scholars, and professionals. It covers mostly intermediate and advanced levels (Master's students to full-time academics) in the academic sphere but is also useful to professionals working in development and business. The book is also of interest to the general public and contributes to the fields of development, business, politics and international relations, conflict resolution and peacebuilding, civil society, and foreign aid. It is a reference book and research monograph to students, experts, and activists who are interested, for example, in Africa, and they might benefit from the experiences of civil society organisations (CSOs) in Sub-Saharan Africa.

The contributors have addressed various issues that may impede CSOs' endeavours, such as resource constraints and coordination challenges. The

DOI: 10.4324/9781003565048-8

contributors, however, explore the significance of government and international relief agencies in delivering help and support in times of humanitarian crises, as civil society organisations (CSOs) in isolation may lack the capability to adequately address the multifaceted needs of the impacted people. The volume has addressed serious militarism and violence challenges on the entire civil society in the Middle East today, owing to ongoing conflict in Palestine and Lebanon, which threaten global peace and security. The authors discussed these issues from the local development and peacebuilding perspectives while EU policies have remained unchanged in terms of current conflict and war. Contemporarily, the dramatic events of the past years, comprising the COVID-19 pandemic, climate change, and the militarisation of international relations, including the Russia–Ukraine war, have violently catapulted the EU into a post-globalisation phase and forced strong empires to return to international relations.

Examples of Threat to Local Ownership of Civil Society

The massive destruction caused by the Israeli military machines imposed real barriers to the civil society in the Gaza Strip, since October 2023. The current war of more than a year while writing these lines now has created a new Nakba for Palestinian families who were displaced more than five times, in the Gaza Strip, during this war. The first Nakba happened for the Palestinians when they were forced to displace and to leave their homes in historical Palestine in 1948, which is today Israel, when it was established by the same policy of destroying their civil society, uprooting their villages, and killing thousands of Palestinians. The current disaster has already made hundreds of thousands of the families displaced, while the Israeli occupation is not allowing them to return to their houses in Gaza city and the north part of the Strip. In this war, Israel killed more than 42,000 and left the families with devastating psychological, social, and financial problems while uncovering mass graves in and around three hospitals in the Gaza Strip.

The current war on the Gaza Strip in response to Hamas attack on southern Israel, on October 7th, 2023, shows Israel's appetite for destroying the Palestinian civil society, not truly hunting Hamas' fighters. Israel targeted indiscriminately hospitals, civil institutions, schools, roads, mosques, cultural sites, very historical places, and churches such as the Orthodox Cultural Centre in Gaza, which was destroyed by the Israeli bombardment; some 500 people took shelter in the Tel al-Hawa neighbourhood in the southern part of the Gaza city. U.N. Secretary-General Antonio Guterres, however, remarks that the Hamas attack on southern Israel, on October 7th, 'did not happen in a vacuum'. Guterres believes the roots of current conflict/war go beyond this date, decades ago, as he said. The UN General secretary said that the international humanitarian law must be respected too. Guterres called repeatedly for a humanitarian ceasefire; however, it was not respected by the Israelis.

All UN and international organisations have documented the war on the Gaza Strip independently, emphasising the current horrific humanitarian disaster facing the Palestinians since October 2023. Not only the Palestinians face these risks alone but also international staff—seven staff members of the Central World Central Kitchen (WCK) were targeted on April 1, 2024, in a targeted attack by Israelis forcing the WCK to suspend operations in the Gaza Strip. Despite the global condemnation for killing them and hindering the access of international media to the Strip, Israeli occupation killed on May 12, *Waibhav Anil Kale*, an Indian national who worked as UN security coordination officer, in Rafah, when their vehicle came under attack. The attacks on the humanitarian organisations as UNRWA have taken various ranges internationally and locally as UNRWA reported on May 13. The Gazans whose houses were destroyed are now seeking shelters as they wait for the aid needed to survive and hopefully, rebuilding the Strip once again.

The entire Palestinian local civil society have been living in inhumane conditions and now rely on donor assistance as they are living in dire circumstances with no access to basic food and water for months while being imposed a full closure under continuous bombardments. The destruction of the Gaza Strip and the resulting humanitarian crisis have put pressure on the international community for a ceasefire first, now. This must be followed by a recovery plan as the destruction of infrastructure is estimated in the first four months of war on Gaza at about $18.5bn. The damage was equivalent to 97% of the combined GDP of the occupied West Bank and Gaza in 2022. "The level of destruction in the Gaza Strip since October 2023 is unprecedented", as per the Interim Damage Assessment report. This war has created a new environment of massive destruction of civil society in terms of schools, hospitals, and institutions. In other words, it has destroyed everything for the Palestinians to live in dignity and peace.

These violations of international law and human rights by the Israeli occupation forces have put pressure on many countries; for example the students' uprisings, which began in the United States and spread to the United Kingdom, France, Switzerland, and Ireland. There has been a massive engagement of civil society groups in public diplomacy campaigns to advocate Palestine's right in existence. More importantly, some of these countries such as Spain and Ireland have taken a way forward to recognise the Palestine state on May 28th, 2024.

This step of recognition was unlike the case of Sweden in 2014. Sweden's recognition has been seen as a symbolic and solidarity gesture and in support for Palestinians' legitimate right in statehood and self-determination after decades of a failed 'peace process' between the Palestinian Liberation Organisations (PLO) and Israel. To what extent has Sweden's formal recognition assisted the Palestinians in their endeavours to achieve their political goals? Sweden recognition came in a time, when the regional order and global polarity were in a different shape, order, and polarity; however, Ireland recognition for Palestine came together with other European countries such as Norway and Spain on May 28th in a highly polar global order including the war on Ukraine while Palestine witnessed a deadly conflict and war on the Gaza Strip since October 2023. To what extent the European states' recognition will help in saving the local civil society from the military aggression and various cycles of conflict, which have destroyed the civil society structure, spreading diseases and impacting the environment including the basic human security needs? These steps have not changed the circumstances on the grounds such as stopping aggression or protecting populations in the occupied territories of Palestine.

The entire civil society of Lebanon is being challenged by Israeli military attacks, which have caused destruction and displacement of civilians since September 2024 while serious threats were imposed on UN peacekeeping forces in South Lebanon. Military attacks and threats imposed a burden on civil society organisations, which are unable to respond to the increasing number of displaced people's demands and needs. Rising service demand has put a strain on the civil society, making it more important than ever to provide additional assistance to vulnerable communities. The conflicts in the region have always put extensive pressure on the entire civil society and the local organisations; for example CSOs assumed a different approach and roles for coordinating responses, identifying new groups' needs, and exploring ways to respond to them owing to the conflict in Syria and the flood of refugees to Jordan during the Syria crisis.

This work introduces a local concept of 'ownership' from an economic development perspective, despite the challenges and restrictions on foreign aid. To what extent has the Syrian conflict affected the scope of work of CSOs in Jordan? How have CSOs challenged the circumstances that emerged owing to the flood of refugees to Jordan? How has it affected the cooperation and partnership between local and international CSOs? In addition, the chapter considers some CSOs/charities from Jordan to identify the differences in the technical, cultural, and political contexts and the social and environmental dynamics that had an impact on their work during COVID-19, as the lockdowns created barriers to effective CSOs. This work also undertakes an examination of the economic consequences, providing valuable insights into the complex equilibrium that must be maintained to ensure that foreign aid favourably impacts Jordan's sustained economic development. Examination of foreign aid for economic development and the significant role of civil society in the local social change process will assist readers to understand a number of factors in this context including the impact of digital technology on local sustainable development and peacebuilding. However, local partners had to employ digital technology tools to coordinate their deliveries in cooperation with the national organisations and other international partners from the 'global north'.

Digital Technology for Local Development

Digital technology has challenged the local ownership concepts and practices of civil society organisations' (CSOs) in their scope of work, operations, and public engagement. CSOs, however, have employed social media platforms to facilitate their operations in responding to donors' conditions and their grassroots demands and needs. The use of technology for tools by CSOs could potentially affect the marginalisation of groups without access to the internet, which risks the domination of social change and community development requirements and conditions. This domination could strengthen CSOs' engagement and their leaders' power over the grassroots, and target groups would benefit more from donor-funded projects in the fields of community development and social change. These perceptions of CSOs and their grassroots movements of local campaigns should not contradict the CSOs' missions in achieving their objective to promote human security and community development processes at different levels.

The mounting pressures impacted on the everyday work of the CSOs and the shifts and challenges they underwent, owing to violence, conflict, and militarism in some countries in the global south. CSOs employed, however, digital technology applications such as Facebook and X (formerly Twitter) to localise their operations and interventions by replacing traditional channels of communication such as in-person meetings and field visits. Violence, conflict, and militarism actions interrupted access to technology as it happened in Palestine and Lebanon in October 2023. In other words, CSOs have realised the significance and impact of technology despite the complexity of accessibility, censorship, cultural contexts, political environment, and social dynamics.

This book also concludes with some implications and offers directions for future research in the field of CSOs' engagement, contributions, and deliveries in non-Western regions. Although societies in the global south have demonstrated resilience, this concludes the presence of structural barriers and systemic inequalities that can impede their capacity to adapt to shifts and changes efficiently.

Way Forward: Small States' Contribution to Global Development

Today, the world is challenged by various crises, wars, and conflicts that shape and affect daily political, financial, and economic circumstances, while competition is increasing among states over domination, power, and resources. More importantly, the great powers have failed to resolve these challenges owing to a number of issues, including the absence of desire and increasing competition; however, some small states have attempted to engage, contribute, or avoid these circumstances. Small states have invested vast resources to protect their interests and increase their engagement, contribution, and benefits at the political and economic levels.

This will provide the reader with not only empirically based and up-to-date but also scientifically grounded analyses of small states' positions, behaviours, and interests caused by various conflicts, militarism, climate change, diseases, and other challenges. It will appeal not only to an academic audience but also to international agencies, policymakers, and practitioners active in the specified regions.

This new research will investigate important questions, including: To what extent have conflict, militarism, climate change, and diseases challenged small states' responses, goals, strategies, shifts, interests, and missions in conflict zones? What are the pros and cons of the impacts of conflict, militarism, climate change, and diseases on small states' responses, engagement, shifts, and challenges? It studies these challenges and how small states have coped with these shifts, and it also examines at least two different positions, behaviours, challenges, responses, and engagements from each country to identify the differences among various contexts, political environments, and economic dynamics to understand these shifts and challenges. For example how have small states responded to the conflicts in Ukraine, Sudan, Niger, Mali, Libya, Yemen, Lebanon, Palestine, Syria, Iraq, the Horn of Africa, etc.? These countries have been enduring very severe circumstances owing to economic declines, food security, energy problems and challenges, external interventions, the absence of reconciliation, violence/militarism, and divisions. These circumstances have already created barriers to international and UN agencies intervening and delivering aid effectively.

This new research will focus on challenges and opportunities facing small states when responding to the current challenges of conflicts, militarism, climate change, and diseases. Many small countries have employed soft power and public diplomacy to intervene in conflicts and wars around the world. Joseph Nye has previously discussed the importance of 'soft power' for small and great powers in achieving their foreign policy goals, and small states use soft power to achieve their foreign policy goals and expand their interests much more effectively than some great powers. Human rights, meanwhile, is a core issue for Western democracies abroad to engage with local societies in the field of human rights at various levels, including reporting political violations committed by local authorities or non-state actors, training civil activists, or reforming and modernising processes and legislation. However, this situation has been challenged by the current global disorder owing to a number of conflicts and wars.

More significantly, states use various foreign aid mechanisms and tools, including CSOs and INGOs, to influence certain countries in the global south. This might include engaging in grassroots cultural, social, and political activities. Small aid and assistance grants are considered public diplomacy activities and accumulated soft power from international donors' perspectives. Small states' cooperation with local CSOs may contribute to relief, community development, and conflict resolution activities in post-conflict consensus-building. This participatory process is also associated with the practice of a top-down mechanism conducted to include citizens' engagement with and contribution to the public sector. The central argument in the investigation of the primary research question (To what extent have conflicts, militarism, climate change, and diseases challenged small states' responses, goals, strategies, shifts, interests, and missions in conflict zones?) is thus contrary to broad assumptions that small states have no room or power to influence world politics or contribute to solving wars and conflict. The following sub-themes may help the researchers to map their thoughts around primary themes:

- Small states' soft power
- Small states' foreign aid and public diplomacy
- Challenges to community development and small states
- Small states' innovations, technology, and development
- Conflict resolution approaches: mediation, intervention, and humanitarian aid
- Small states' cybersecurity threats, challenges, and opportunities
- Economic power of small states
- Small states' foreign policy opportunities and challenges
- Small states' economic diplomacy
- Small countries, food security, and the energy crisis
- Small states' intervention in sectarianism, militarism, and violence
- Small countries' contributions to the humanitarian crisis
- Small states, COVID-19, climate change, and diseases

In brief, CSOs have a vital role in providing support and empowerment to communities in the global south during times of crisis. Through close collaboration with policymakers and conducting in-depth research, CSOs can effectively tackle the distinct challenges encountered by these societies. In the future, CSOs must persist in their efforts to champion the rights of marginalised communities and strive for enhanced social justice and equality globally. Success in effectively navigating the complex and ever-changing landscape of global development requires equal partnership, continuous collaboration, and innovation in reference to sustainable development goals.

Index

For Product Safety Concerns and Information please contact our EU representative GPSR@taylorandfrancis.com
Taylor & Francis Verlag GmbH, Kaufingerstraße 24, 80331 München, Germany

www.ingramcontent.com/pod-product-compliance
Lightning Source LLC
LaVergne TN
LVHW010932110826
845149LV00013B/2561

9781032932439